A FRESH LOOK AT THE BOOK OF JONAH

A FRESH LOOK AT THE BOOK OF JONAH

THE HARD-TO-SWALLOW TRUTH ABOUT DISOBEDIENCE

GREG LAURIE

A Fresh Look at the Book of Jonah: The Hard-to-Swallow Truth About Disobedience

Art direction: Greg Laurie
Art production: Mark Ferjulian
Cover design: Ty Mattson
Copy Editor: Karla Pedrow

ISBN 978-0-9916518-3-2

Cataloging-in-Publication Data is available.

1 2 3 4 5 6 7 8 / 19 18 17 16 15 14

CONTENTS

CHAPTER 1
HERE AM I . . . SEND HIM!

Have you ever heard the story of Wrong Way Roy?

Actually, his name was Roy Riegels, an All-American center for the University of California, Berkeley Golden Bears who were facing Georgia Tech in the 1929 Rose Bowl. In addition to playing center on offense, Roy also played what was known as a roving center on defense, similar to today's middle linebacker. Midway through the second quarter, with Georgia Tech on offense on their own thirty, one of the Tech players fumbled the ball.

Riegels alertly scooped it up and began to sprint toward the end zone, some sixty-nine yards away.

But there was one problem. It was the wrong end zone. If Roy had succeeded, he would have scored a touchdown for the opposing team.

Riegels later told the Associated Press, "I was running toward the sidelines when I picked up the ball. I started to my left toward Tech's goal. Somebody shoved me, and I bounded right off into a tackler. In pivoting to get away from him, I completely lost my bearings."

Watching with disbelief from the sideline, Georgia Tech coach Bill Alexander told his players, "Sit down. Sit down. He's just running the wrong way. Every step he takes is to our advantage."

Fortunately, Benny Lom, one of his Cal teammates, caught up with Riegels before he got across the wrong goal line. Even so, Tech ended up scoring a safety before halftime and went into the locker rooms leading 2-0.

In the Cal locker room, the distraught Riegels initially refused to even return to the game for the second half. He told his coach, Nibs Price, "Coach, I can't do it. I've ruined you, I've ruined myself, I've ruined the University of California. I couldn't face that crowd to save my life."

But Price told him, "Roy, get up and go back out there—the game is only half over."[1] Riegels did go back for the second half and turned in one of the most inspiring efforts in Rose Bowl history.

Have you ever felt like Wrong Way Roy?

Maybe at some point in your life, the Lord told you to go one direction, and you deliberately went in the other direction. Perhaps at this very moment you are running from God's purposes and plans for your life.

The Bible never records whether or not the prophet Jonah had a nickname. But if he'd had one, it might very well have been Wrong Way Jonah.

God clearly and specifically called him in one direction, and in response he booked passage on a ship heading in an opposite direction.

Jonah found out, as we will see in the pages of this little book, that although you might run from God, you really can't hide. But the prophet would also find out something else: that God gives second chances, even when we fail.

Newsflash: Fish Bites Man

Whenever most people hear the name *Jonah*, they immediately think of Jonah and the whale or Jonah and the great fish.

It's sort of like eating sushi in reverse. Instead of man eating fish, we have a fish eating man. In reality, however, only three verses of the book of Jonah deal with the fish. As G. Campbell Morgan pointed out, "Men have been looking so hard at the great fish that they have failed to see the great God."

Some people, of course, struggle with the whole premise of someone being swallowed by a fish and living to tell the story.

I don't think it's difficult at all. If you believe Genesis 1:1, that "in the beginning God created the heavens and the earth," you can believe this story as well.

But the most important reason for believing in the account of Jonah and the great fish is that it was validated by Jesus Christ Himself. In Matthew 12:38, some of the Pharisees and teachers of the law came to Jesus, demanding a miraculous sign from Him. In verses 39-41 Jesus replied,

> "An evil and adulterous generation seeks after a sign, and no sign will be given to it except the sign of the prophet Jonah. For as Jonah was three days and three nights in the belly of the great fish, so will the Son of Man be three days and three nights in the heart of the earth. The men of Nineveh will rise up in the judgment with this generation and condemn it, because they repented at the preaching of Jonah; and indeed a greater than Jonah is here."

Not only did Christ validate the story, but He used it to illustrate His own death and resurrection.

What an amazing prophet Jonah was. The place from which he prophesied was the bottom of the sea, and the pulpit from which he preached was the stomach of a fish. This is the story of a man who was given a mission to perform and a task to accomplish who (at first) flatly refused to obey. But thankfully, it is also a story of God's longsuffering, patience, and willingness to forgive those who stop running from Him and begin to run toward Him instead.

God Said, "Go" . . . Jonah Said, "No"

The book of Jonah could be summed up this way.

God said, "Go."

Jonah said, "No."

God said, "Oh?"

Remember this: God always will have the last word.

I find it interesting that it took God longer to prepare His servant to obey His call than it did for the entire godless city of Nineveh to repent.

Have things changed all that much? Not really. As our evangelistic team goes into various communities preparing for citywide Harvest crusades, it seems like our biggest, most challenging task is to get pastors and churches to simply talk to each other. In many communities, there is virtually no communication between churches. Then, after we get the churches talking to one another, the next challenge is to get them to pray together. It always amazes me how hard we have to work at trying to convince pastors and Christians of the importance of the Great Commission.

We are living in a day when the church is awash in conferences, concerts, and worship times, and I enthusiastically support all of those things. But the simple fact is, Jesus didn't command us to go into all the world and have conferences or concerts. But He *did* command us to go into all the world and preach the gospel.

That is God's unmistakable call to us today, just as He clearly called Jonah to declare His message in that prophet's generation.

The Call of Jonah

Here, then, is how the call of God came to Jonah:

> Now the word of the Lord came to Jonah the son of Amittai, saying, "Arise, go to Nineveh, that great city, and cry out against it; for their wickedness has come up before Me." But Jonah arose to flee to Tarshish from the presence of the LORD. He went down to Joppa, and found a ship going to Tarshish; so he paid the fare, and went down into it, to go with them to Tarshish from the presence of the LORD. (Jonah 1:1-3)

Before you find yourself quickly condemning Jonah for his stubborn disobedience, it might be good to ask yourself, "Have I ever tried to run from God and His will for my life?"

Maybe, like Wrong Way Roy, you have been going in the wrong direction, thinking you had a better, more logical plan for your life than God does. Maybe there were certain truths in the Scriptures that you simply didn't want to face up to or follow. God might have placed a clear calling on your life to do something, and you simply didn't want to do it.

That was Jonah's issue. Even though he was a prophet of God, he *did not*, under any circumstances, want to bring God's word to the city of Nineveh.

What do we know about this city?

When I was in London a number of years ago, I visited one of their great museums and looked at actual artifacts from the city of Nineveh. Nineveh was once one of the greatest cities in the history of the earth. The walls of Nineveh were so wide that three chariots could be driven abreast over them. The city had streets that were twenty miles long and walls that were one hundred feet high. By any standards, it was a massive, very impressive city.

It was big in another way, too.

It was big in sin. Nineveh was renowned for its wickedness. God even comments on it in verse 2: "For their wickedness has come up before Me." A literal translation reads, "Their wickedness has reached a high degree or the highest pitch." Like an overflowing septic tank, Nineveh stunk to high heaven. This verse shows that God is acutely aware of the wickedness of man. We might imagine that He tunes out all the evil, perversion, and injustice in our world, but in truth, His eyes don't miss one thing.

What kind of people lived in Nineveh?

Very wicked ones. The Ninevites were renowned for their

cruelty. The prophet Nahum gave this gripping description:

> See the flashing swords and glittering spears
> as the charioteers charge past!
> There are countless casualties,
> heaps of bodies—
> so many bodies that
> people stumble over them.
> All this because Nineveh,
> the beautiful and faithless city,
> mistress of deadly charms,
> enticed the nations with her beauty.
> She taught them all her magic,
> enchanting people everywhere.
> (Nahum 3:3-4, NLT)

The prophet acknowledged that Nineveh was a beautiful city but also a very wicked city, with literal piles of bodies in the streets. The Ninevites were known for their savagery in plundering cities—burning boys and girls alive and torturing adults, tearing the skin from their bodies, and leaving them to die in the scorching sun.

In the ruins of ancient Nineveh, archaeologists have actually discovered monuments that were built by various individuals to their atrocities. One of those monuments says, "I cut the limbs off the officers who rebelled."

Another monument states, "Within the border of my own land, I flayed and spread their skins upon the walls." In other words, these people were skinned alive, and the skins of the people were hung on the walls.

Another cruel Ninevite wrote, "I cut off their hands and their fingers, and from others I cut off their noses and ears and fingers. For many of them, I put out their eyes."

These were wicked, depraved people—the Nazis or al Qaeda of their own era.

And God was sending Jonah to preach to them.

From Jonah's perspective, this was an outrageous assignment on several levels. First of all, Jonah was a Jew, and the Ninevites were the avowed enemies of Israel. Asking Jonah to travel to the capital city of the Assyrians and preach to the Ninevites would have been like asking a Jew living in the Warsaw ghetto in World War II to travel to Berlin and hold a crusade for the Nazis. Or, it would be like going to an Israeli today and saying, "Go and preach to the nation of Iran, because I'm going to judge them if you don't."

A loyal Israeli might reply, "Good! Go ahead and judge them! These are the people who say they want to wipe Israel off the face of the earth."

God's actual words to Jonah were, "Arise, go to Nineveh." A literal translation would read, "Get up and go."

So Jonah got up and went . . . in the wrong direction. Instead of going five hundred miles northeast to Nineveh,

Jonah attempted to go two thousand miles west to Tarshish—about as far from Nineveh as you could travel in those days.

Maybe that's true of you as you read these words. You're in a boat headed for Tarshish when you know in your heart that God has said, "Go to Nineveh."

Two Roads

There are two roads in life. One road leads to Nineveh. The other road leads to Tarshish. One road is the will of God. The other is disobedience to His will.

Which road are you on? Are you on the road to disobedience or on the road to obedience? Are you doing what God has asked you to do, or are you resisting and rebelling against what He has asked you do?

Why was Jonah so dead set against going to Nineveh? What was the real reason? There are several possibilities.

Maybe it was because he thought he would be unpopular—or even in danger of his life—in that city. He would most likely be a lone Jew in a city that thoroughly despised Jews. He might have said to himself, "Maybe they'll gouge out my eyes or flay me alive and hang my skin on the wall."

Then again, maybe Jonah didn't want to go because he simply didn't care. He really wasn't concerned about Nineveh—its people or its children. He didn't care about their plight or impending judgment. He might have thought, *Serves them right. Anyway, it's not my problem.*

Maybe he didn't want to do it because the task seemed so difficult. It was a long, possibly dangerous overland journey to the Assyrian capital. The days and days of travel by foot or perhaps on the back of a donkey would have seemed inconvenient at best and downright arduous at the worst.

But there is a fourth possibility, which I believe to be the real reason Jonah didn't want to go to Nineveh: *he didn't want to go because he was certain his mission would succeed*. Deep down, he knew that if he preached to those people, they would repent, and God would forgive them and give them a second chance.

He didn't want them to have a second chance.

In Jonah 4:2, after the prophet's worst fears were confirmed and God had spared the great city, Jonah complained bitterly to the Lord, saying, "This is exactly what I thought you'd do, Lord, when I was there in my own country and you first told me to come here. That's why I ran away to Tarshish. For I knew you were a gracious God, merciful, slow to get angry, and full of kindness; I knew how easily you could cancel your plans for destroying these people" (TLB).

Sometimes people will say, "I have a problem with the God of the Old Testament. He is wrathful and angry, cruel and mean. I believe in the God of the New Testament, who is compassionate, loving, and gracious."

Here's a newsflash: the God of the Old Testament is gracious and loving, and the God of the New Testament is just and righteous. I believe in the God of the Old and the New Testament because *He is the same God.* He is full of mercy and love.

The bottom line is that Jonah wanted God to take out Nineveh. He wanted these people to be eliminated. In fact, he even enjoyed the idea of their being wiped out.

If we were really honest, we would acknowledge that we have probably shared that same attitude at times. Though we wouldn't admit it (out loud), we might take a perverse pleasure in knowing that certain people who bother us or annoy us are going to hell. Where in the world do we get such an attitude? It certainly doesn't come from God!

The fact is, we *all* deserve God's judgment. Jesus didn't say to hate your enemies and hope that judgment comes upon them. Rather, He said, "Love your enemies, bless those who curse you, do good to those who hate you, and pray for those who spitefully use you and persecute you" (Matthew 5:44).

Is there someone whom you would actually like to see go to hell? Maybe it's your boss. Maybe it's your husband. Maybe it's a neighbor who drives you crazy. Maybe it's someone who once hurt you deeply. And yes, truly, this person might be headed for hell. But that should break your heart rather than give you any satisfaction.

The reason Jonah didn't want to go to Nineveh was because he was a racist. He was a patriotic Israeli who hated the Ninevites, and he didn't want them to believe.

A racist? Our contemporary culture throws around this term way too freely. People are called "racists" or "bigots" for just about any reason—or for no reason at all. In actuality, a real racist or bigot is a person who hates an entire race of people.

That is what Jonah was. He wanted the Ninevites—all of them—to be eliminated. He strongly suspected that God might have mercy on them, holding back His hand of wrath, and that made him furious.

The Great Commission and the Call of Jonah

God had told Jonah, "Go to the great city of Nineveh and preach against it, because its wickedness has come up before me" (1:2, NIV).

Go and *preach.* In the original Hebrew, those words are in the imperative. In other words, God wasn't offering a suggestion here; this was a direct command. From our vantage point thousands of years later, we look back on this story and say, "Jonah should have obeyed." But guess what? *Jesus has said the same thing to us.*

We call it the Great Commission, and it is found in Matthew 28:19-20, where Jesus says, "Go therefore and make disciples of all the nations, baptizing them in the name of the Father and of the Son and of the Holy Spirit, teaching them to observe all things that I have commanded you."

There are two things to note about the Great Commission that remind us of the call to Jonah.

1. It is a command.

Again, we don't call these words from Jesus the Great Suggestion; it is the Great Commission. For too many, the Great Commission has become the Great Omission.

The commission of the church isn't to wait until the world shows up on its doorstep; the commission of the church is to go to the whole world. But let's personalize that a little. If you belong to Jesus Christ, *you* are the church. Are you going into all the world with the good news about Jesus? Are you going into your sphere of influence, expressing to your friends, family, neighbors, and workplace what Jesus has done for you? Or are you more like Jonah, knowing what you ought to do but running in the opposite direction instead?

2. It is addressed to every follower of Jesus.

By the way, our Lord's words in Matthew 28 were addressed to every one of His followers—not just the so-called professionals like pastors, evangelists, and missionaries. These words were given to every follower of Jesus, to every business professional, to every homemaker, to every student, to every grandfather and grandmother, to every young boy and girl. Those words are a commission given to us by Christ Himself. If I am His disciple, then I am commanded to go and make disciples of others. *Are you doing your part?*

It's interesting to me that Jesus spoke these words of the Great Commission at the very end of His earthly ministry. It was almost like an exclamation point. Sometimes we will hear people say that the last words of Christ were from the cross. And yes, those were His last words before He died. Afterward, however, He rose from the dead and walked once again among His followers on earth. But He spoke the Great Commission immediately prior to His being caught up into heaven (see Acts 1:8-11).

If someone close to you is about to leave you for a long time, you just naturally pay closer attention to his or her parting words. Why? Because those will be the most important words on that person's heart—and they will be words that he or she wants you to remember. In the Great Commission, Jesus in essence is saying, "These are my closing thoughts. Listen carefully, because these are the words that need to echo in your ears from now on."

In my opinion, to be careless about carrying out this commission is a sin.

Someone might say, "A sin? Really, Greg? I think you're going too far."

Even so, I would call it a *sin of omission.* James 4:17 says, "Therefore, to him who knows to do good and does not do it, to him it is sin."

Chuck Swindoll tells the story of a man who was walking along a boat dock in Boston Harbor when he suddenly tripped over a rope and fell into the deep water. He came up sputtering and calling for help, only to sink again. It was obvious that he didn't know how to swim and that he was in serious trouble. His friends were too far away and didn't even hear his cries.

Meanwhile, only a few yards away, a young man was lying on the dock, sunbathing. He heard the man in distress, crying out, "Help! I'm drowning! I can't swim!" As it turned out, the young sunbather was an excellent swimmer. But instead of jumping into the harbor to save the drowning man, he only turned his head to watch as the man went down for the last time and disappeared beneath the water.

The family of the man who died was so outraged by this calloused indifference that they sued the sunbather. The court, however, ruled that the man on the dock had no legal responsibility whatsoever to try and save the other man's life. In so ruling, the court agreed with the murderer Cain, who said to the Lord, "Am I my brother's keeper?" (Genesis 4:9).

Chuck Swindoll concluded with this statement: "Indifference may not be illegal, but it is immoral."[2]

When we encounter people who don't know Jesus or the way of salvation, and we have the opportunity to give them the answer that will save them but choose not to, are we any different from the sunbather who let the man drown? We need to take advantage of every opportunity the Lord opens up for us. We need to say, "Friend, let me pull you out of the water. Let me tell you about Jesus. Let me invite you to Christ."

In one way, ignoring someone who needs Christ is even worse than letting a man drown just yards away from us. Neglecting to tell someone about Jesus has eternal ramifications.

In Mark's version of the Great Commission, Jesus said, "Go into all the world and preach the gospel" (Mark 16:15). Notice that Jesus did *not* say, "Go into all the world and be good examples." And truly, we should be good examples; we certainly don't want to be bad ones. The fact is, if you are a good example of Christlike living, you may very well earn the right to share the gospel with someone. But the Great Commission is not about being a good example. The Great Commission is a clear command to verbalize the gospel—to communicate it.

Why do I bring this up? Because some people will say, "I'm not really comfortable with bringing these subjects up with people. It's too confrontational. I would rather just live my life and win them over by being a good example."

But you won't.

Men and women will not be won to Christ merely by your example.

Hopefully, the way you live your life will build a bridge to their lives so that you will have the opportunity to share the message of salvation with them. *But being a good example is not enough.* The gospel is good news, and it's something that you have to announce. Can you imagine a news anchor on TV who decided to just live the news or be a good example of the news instead of actually announcing the news on camera? People would call that station and say, "Listen, being a good example is fine. We appreciate that. But we need you to *tell* us the news so that we can know what's going on in the world."

In the same way, we are called to deliver the good news, not just sit there and expect people to watch our lives. We are to *engage people* with the message of salvation in Christ.

How does God choose to primarily reach nonbelievers?

Through the preaching of the gospel.

In 1 Corinthians 1:21 Paul wrote, "For since, in the wisdom of God, the world through wisdom did not know God, it pleased God through the foolishness of the message preached to save those who believe."

In other words, God has chosen verbal communication.

Now if I were God, I would never use people at all to reach other people—and I certainly would never use me. I once heard J. Vernon McGee say to his congregation, "If you knew me as well I as I know me, you wouldn't be sitting there listening to me right now!" Then, after a pause, he continued, "But if I knew *you* as well as you know you, I wouldn't want to preach to you!"

How true. In the same way, if you knew me as well as I know me, you probably wouldn't be reading my book right now. We are all very flawed people. As the apostle James wrote, "We all stumble in many ways" (James 3:2, NIV).

Even so, God has determined to use people to reach people.

If it were up to me, I would say, "Forget people! I'm going to use angels to preach the gospel." After all, angels are powerful, holy, awesome, and radiant with beauty. And if that weren't enough, I could instruct them to pull out a sword while they were speaking, just for effect. But again, in God's wisdom, He has given the job of announcing salvation to regular, fallible human beings. As Paul wrote in Romans 10:14, "How, then, can they call on the one they have not believed in? And how can they believe in the one of whom they have not heard? And how can they hear without someone preaching to them?" (NIV).

That is the whole point in a nutshell, isn't it?

How can they hear without someone preaching to them?

Jonah understood these principles very well. He understood how effective preaching God's message could be. But because he hated Nineveh, he deliberately turned his back on God's call and fled in the opposite direction.

You Can't Hide from God

Jonah 1:3 tells us that "Jonah arose to flee to Tarshish from the presence of the LORD."

Here's another newsflash: you cannot escape God's presence. No one can. The Bible tells us that God is present everywhere. We call this the *omnipresence* of God.

In Jonah's time, Israel already had the complete book of Psalms. It makes me wonder, did Jonah ever read the words of King David in Psalm 139:7-10?

> Where can I go from Your Spirit?
> Or where can I flee from Your presence?
> If I ascend into heaven, You are there;
> If I make my bed in hell, behold, You are there.
> If I take the wings of the morning,
> And dwell in the uttermost parts of the sea,
> Even there Your hand shall lead me,
> And Your right hand shall hold me.

You can't escape from God or hide from His presence. But that won't stop people from trying. Back in the Garden of Eden, Adam and Eve tried to hide from God after they had committed the first sin and ate of the forbidden fruit. After sewing little aprons of fig leaves together to hide their nakedness, they actually ducked behind some trees when they heard God walking in the Garden in the cool of the day.

The Lord called out, "Where are you?"

Why did God do that? Had He really lost Adam's location? Not a chance. He knew exactly where Adam was, and He also knew what Adam had done.

It reminds me of when I play hide-and-seek with my grandchildren. They run and hide, and I always know where they are. They're not very good at deception yet. They will hide behind the curtains, but I can see their little feet. Or they will start giggling, and all I have to do is follow the giggles. Sometimes I will find them in the very same hiding place they had just used. But part of the game is that I act like I don't know where they are and keep calling out to them. Then they jump out of their hiding places and yell at me, and I act startled and scared.

Adam and Eve may have thought they were hiding in the trees, but they never were out of sight from the Lord for even a second. You can't flee from the presence of God, no matter where you go.

In the book of Jeremiah, God asked the prophet, "Can anyone hide from me in a secret place? Am I not everywhere in all the heavens and earth?" (Jeremiah 23:24, NLT).

Even so, even though Jonah probably knew deep down that hiding from God was impossible, he still determined to try. And the Devil was right there to cooperate with him.

When the Devil Opens Doors

> But Jonah arose to flee to Tarshish from the presence of the Lord. He went down to Joppa, and found a ship going to Tarshish. (Jonah 1:3)

God isn't the only one who opens doors. Sometimes when events work out for us in a certain way, we will say, "The door is open."

But here's the question: Who opened that door? Was it the Lord? Are you sure?

The fact is, if you are a Christian woman who is struggling in her marriage, you shouldn't be surprised if you meet a compassionate, understanding man who will "give you counsel" about how to deal with your husband. But of course it's a trap. That is not a door God has opened at all.

If you're a single Christian man or woman looking for romance, there always will be a nonbeliever who wants to go out with you.

If you're in a fever to make a pile of money in a hurry, there always will be a get-rich-quick scheme within reach. All you have to do is cut a few corners, tell a few lies, and neglect to disclose certain key points of information, and there's that open door you'd hoped for.

The Devil always will open the doors for you to go in the wrong direction.

You may find your ship, and it may sail right on time. But if you are en route to Tarshish when God has called you to Nineveh, I want you to know something: *There's a storm brewing on the horizon.* And before too long, you'll go overboard. Why? Because God loves you, and He's not going to allow His child to go astray. He will pursue you.

The text says that this runaway prophet "found a ship going to Tarshish; so he paid the fare, and went down into it."

He went down.

And he paid the fare.

Sin is very expensive. If you run away from God, you will always pay your own fare, and you'll never get where you thought you were going when you step off the pier into that boat. It's not going to work out the way you were hoping.

Every step away from God is a step down.

First Jonah went down to Joppa.

Then he went down into the ship.

Then he went down into the sea.

Then he went down into the fish's belly.

Then he went down into the deep.

That is the life of running from God. Running from God is a downer. Don't do it.

King David discovered this. He started going down when he laid lustful eyes on the beautiful Bathsheba as she was bathing herself. He went a little further down when he summoned her to his palace. Then he went down further still when he committed the sin of adultery with her. He went down even further when he murdered her husband Uriah and down yet again when he tried to cover his sin. He went down, down, and down until he repented. And it all started with an unguarded glance that became a lustful gaze.

God, however, always will have the last word. He did with David, and He did with Jonah as well.

Are you running from God?

Resisting His Call

Even as you read these words, you may know in your heart that you are running from God. You're doing things in your life that you know you shouldn't be doing as a follower of Jesus Christ. In effect, you're going to Tarshish when you ought to be taking steps toward Nineveh.

Then again, you might be running from God's call on your life. The Lord has told you to preach the gospel, but you have replied, "I'm kind of busy right now. I'm really not sure if that's something I ought to do."

The Lord has prompted you to bring His message of salvation to your family . . . your coworker . . . your friend . . . your neighbor. But you have said, "I really don't want to do that. I don't want people to think of me as some kind of fanatic."

No matter how you might be running from the Lord or trying to hide from His presence, the good news is this: God loves you, and He is calling you to Himself. He is a God of grace and forgiveness, and He will give you another chance to find His very best for your life.

CHAPTER 2
THE HARD-TO-SWALLOW TRUTH ABOUT DISOBEDIENCE

A young girl stood on a street corner sharing her faith one day, and a small crowd gathered to listen to her.

As she was speaking from the heart about what Christ had done for her, a man who considered himself an intellectual atheist approached. The young woman's words nettled him, and he decided to make her look silly and foolish.

After listening for a while, he interrupted her. "Excuse me, young lady," he bellowed. "I have a question for you."

"Yes sir?" she replied.

"Do you believe the Bible is true?"

"Of course, sir," she said. "I do believe the Bible. I believe every word of it."

"Oh, is that so? And do you believe that all of the miracles in the Bible are true?"

"Yes, sir, I do. I believe they are true.

"That's interesting," the atheist said, beginning to enjoy himself. "So then, you must believe in the story of Jonah and the great fish—that a man was swallowed by a fish and survived to tell the story. Do you believe that?"

"Yes," she said. "It's in the Bible, and I believe it."

Her antagonist had a sneer in his voice. "Then why don't you tell me how such a thing is possible?"

With everyone looking at her, she replied, "I don't know how it's possible. When I get to Heaven, I will ask Jonah."

"Ha!" her antagonist laughed. "And what if he ended up in hell?"

"Well," she said, "maybe *you* could ask him."

Here's the problem with the book of Jonah. We focus so much on the whale or great fish in the story that I think we miss the forest for the trees. The essential message of Jonah is not about a fish. In fact, only three verses deal with the fish. This is really a story about a man who was given a job to do by God and refused to do it. However, because God loved His servant, He wouldn't let Jonah off the hook. After the Lord got his attention, Jonah finally obeyed, and a massive revival took place.

The real message of the book of Jonah is that God gives second chances.

Three Kinds of Storms

Jonah got on a ship heading toward Tarshish—which was the opposite direction from Nineveh.

Someone has said, "Sin always will take you farther than you want to go, keep you longer than you want to stay, and cost you more than you want to spend."

But the book of Jonah reminds us that God always will have the last word. Here is how the story unfolded for the disobedient prophet:

> But the LORD sent out a great wind on the sea, and there was a mighty tempest on the sea, so that the ship was about to be broken up.
>
> Then the mariners were afraid; and every man cried out to his god, and threw the cargo that was in the ship into the sea, to lighten the load. But Jonah had gone down into the lowest parts of the ship, had lain down, and was fast asleep. (Jonah 1:4-5)

Verse 4 tells us that God sent a great wind—a mighty storm—to get the attention of the prodigal prophet.

All of us will face storms in life. It is something that no one escapes. Jesus Himself said, "In the world you will have tribulation" (John 16:33). Peter reminds us not to be surprised or taken aback when hardship or trials come our way (1 Peter 4:12).

Warren Wiersbe has pointed out that there are two kinds of storms we encounter as followers of Christ: storms of *correction* and storms of *perfection*.[1] I would also suggest a third category: storms of *protection*. I think of them as *correcting, perfecting,* and *protecting* storms.

First, there are *correcting* storms.

That is the kind of storm in which Jonah found himself. A *correcting* storm is one we usually bring upon ourselves. We reap what we sow, experiencing the consequences of our own actions.

We could compare it to a husband's reaction to his failing marriage. He moans and wrings his hands. "Why is this happening to me?" he says. "Why has this storm come into our lives?"

We might reply to him, "Perhaps it's because you have been a poor excuse for a husband for years and haven't loved your wife as Christ loves the church, as Ephesians 5:25 tells us. You have effectively brought this storm upon yourself."

This was a storm intended to get Jonah's attention. As a child of God, Jonah was experiencing God's hand of discipline, or chastening. It was a reminder to Jonah that the Lord loved him and still wanted to use him.

How do we know that God loves us? Because we feel it all the time? No, because we won't experience those warm and fuzzy emotions day in and day out. The most obvious way we can know that God loves us is by remembering that He sent His Son to the cross for us, dying in our place for our sins.

But He also shows that He loves us through His discipline. In fact, the Lord says that whom He loves He disciplines. In Hebrews 12:6-8 we read,

> "For the LORD disciplines those he loves, and he punishes each one he accepts as his child."
>
> As you endure this divine discipline, remember that God is treating you as his own children. Who ever heard of a child who is never disciplined by its father? If God doesn't discipline you as he does all of his children, it means that you are illegitimate and are not really his children at all. (NLT)

If you go through your growing-up years without discipline, then you have parents who are failing in their God-given task. That was pretty much the story of my childhood and, sadly, it's the story of far too many children in America today.

I grew up without a father and with a mom who was frequently absent. I had no rule, no curfews, no discipline, no set bedtime, and no expectation of good grades or good behavior. There were no homecooked meals. Every night I would go out to a local coffee shop and order the same thing: a hamburger, a vanilla shake, and fries. That was what I ate every night. My friends all told me, "You are so lucky! We have to go home and sit down at the table with our parents and eat the food they serve us. We wish we could live your life."

But guess what? I wish I could have lived their lives. I got tired of hamburgers, fries, and vanilla shakes, but that's about all I knew to order. In time, I started going over to a friend's house and sitting down at a family meal with him, along with his mom and dad. I ate food that I didn't even like because I longed for some structure in my life. I wanted family because I didn't have it. The truth is, I would have *welcomed* a little parental discipline. It would have at least shown me that someone cared for me enough to check up on me.

Because Jonah was God's loved child, he was disciplined. The Lord sent him into a great storm and crisis to remind him that he was loved. God was saying to him, "I'm not finished with you yet, Jonah."

Maybe God has allowed a storm to come into your life to get your attention. The Bible tells us that "all we like sheep have gone astray" (Isaiah 53:6). Maybe, even as a believer, you have wandered away from Him, and He has been calling you to come back. If His warnings go unheeded, He may allow difficult circumstances to come into your life to open your eyes and get you headed back in the right direction again.

The psalmist said, "Before I was afflicted I went astray, but now I obey your word" (Psalm 119:67, NIV). Maybe the

Lord has allowed some difficulty or trial into your life to bring you back to your senses and restore you to a relationship with Him. That is what He was about to do with Jonah.

Second, there are *perfecting* storms.

These are storms that come into our lives at inexplicable times and in inexplicable ways. Joseph faced one of those storms when he was betrayed by his brothers into slavery—and then falsely accused of rape in the home of his new Egyptian master. These false charges were followed by a jail term in an Egyptian dungeon.

Though Joseph couldn't have known it at the time, God was in the midst of refining Joseph's character, molding him into the man He wanted him to be. When the time was right, God vaulted this still-young man into a position of great authority and responsibility. In fact, Joseph, the son of a sheep rancher, would become the second most powerful man in all of the world. Years later, Joseph would find it in his heart to forgive his brothers who had done him such a terrible wrong and reached out to help them and their families.

Maybe you are in the midst of one of those *perfecting* storms right now. God is stretching you, deepening you, and refining your character. In His time, He will bring you through that storm into a place of greater influence in His kingdom.

Third, there are *protecting* storms.

We have an example of this type of storm immediately following Jesus' most popular miracle: the feeding of the five thousand (plus women and children) with the loaves and fishes. After that great sign, the people were so excited that they wanted to immediately seize Jesus and make Him their king—whether He wanted to be or not.

It's easy to imagine that the disciples were as excited as everyone else. The Scriptures make it clear that even after Jesus had died and rose again, they still imagined that He would set up an earthly kingdom (see Acts 1:6). When they heard all the people clamoring to make Jesus king, they might have thought, *Wow, this is great! We've almost reached our goal.*

That's when Jesus put them on a boat on the Sea of Galilee and sent them into a great storm. He later joined them in the middle of the lake after walking to them on the water.

Why had He sent them away at that moment, giving them something to occupy their minds and their strength? One reason is that He might have been protecting them from a big crowd of people with the wrong idea. All of the "let's make Jesus king right now" talk wasn't good for His disciples.

High Seas

I don't know whether you have ever been at sea in the midst of a bad storm. I have, and I don't like it one bit. I'm not one who gets seasick easily, but when I do . . . well, it's pretty miserable. The ship is pitching back and forth, the wind is howling, and I feel like I am going to turn myself inside out with nausea.

Jonah, however, tucked away somewhere down below deck, seemed to be peacefully sleeping through the great storm. To me, this is a picture of the church in our world today. The world is afraid, and the church is asleep. The world is asking questions, and the church often doesn't have answers. People are dying in their sins, and the church is out of the action, unaware, and semicomatose.

You say, "I resent that, Greg. I don't think that I am asleep."

Sometimes you can fall asleep without realizing it. Have you ever sat down on the couch to watch a little TV—and then discover that you've been asleep for an hour? You look at your watch and say, "What happened?" Turning to your spouse, you ask, "Was I sleeping?"

"Yes, you were," your spouse tells you. "You've been out for an hour—and snoring too!"

But you didn't even know it.

Sometimes (for whatever reason) we deny that we've

been sleeping. Maybe someone calls us at 3:00 a.m., and of course their first question is, "Did I wake you up?"

"Oh no. I was awake."

You were awake at 3:00 a.m.? Really? Probably not. (Why do we lie about that?)

It's also true that many people are spiritually asleep, don't realize it, and probably would deny it. You and I can become lethargic when it comes to doing the job that God has called us to do.

I don't know about you, but I get very sleepy after a large meal. Usually after a Thanksgiving dinner, I go into something that could be best described as a food coma.

So, here is something to consider.

An older believer may be in greater danger of sleeping spiritually than a younger believer. The mature saint who has fed on the Word of God for years without a spiritual outlet can fall into a spiritual lethargy more easily than the person who is new to the faith. Most new converts know very well how weak and vulnerable they are and how much they need to learn. As a result, they cling to Jesus, staying as close to Him as they can.

In contrast, sometimes older, more mature Christians may be in spiritual cruise control, feeling as though they already know it all. As a result, they doze off in their spiritual lives and place themselves and their loved ones at great risk.

Jonah was a living, breathing prophet and spokesman for the God of Israel. Even Jesus acknowledged that. Yet there he was, in a time of great crisis and need, sleeping when he should have been praying.

What had God told Jonah to do? Go and preach to the Ninevites. But what was he actually doing? Sleeping soundly in a ship that was headed in the opposite direction.

What has the Lord told you to do? What has the Lord told me to do? He has told us to go into all the world and preach the gospel. If you are not doing that, then you are effectively asleep like Jonah.

In the Phillips translation of Romans 13 we are told, "Why all this stress on behaviour? Because, as I think you have realised, the present time is of the highest importance—it is time to wake up to reality. Every day brings God's salvation nearer. The night is nearly over, the day has almost dawned. Let us therefore fling away the things that men do in the dark, let us arm ourselves for the fight of the day!" (verses 11-13).

In other words, we need to wake up and suit up and do the job that God has called us to do. This isn't an option or an elective. It's a command from the Lord Himself.

God Talk in a Crisis

What a storm that must have been! As the situation grew

more and more dire, Jonah 1:5 tells us that "every man cried out to his god." None of them had the *right* god, but they all cried out to their various deities.

Theirs was an emergency religion. We've all heard the expression, "There are no atheists in foxholes." I think there actually may be a few, but I doubt if there are very many. When crisis hits, people say, "Oh my God!" It's almost like a kneejerk reaction.

It's a good thing to cry out to God, providing that you really want His help—and are crying out to the right God. On board that merchant ship bound for Tarshish, not one of those distressed and fearful sailors had a relationship with the only true God who could save them. Only one man on board had a relationship like that. . . . But he was asleep.

The sailors knew very well that this was no ordinary storm. Something about its sudden approach or it's incredible ferocity told them this went beyond a bad turn in the weather. To find out the cause of this strange and frightening event, they cast lots (we would say they drew straws) and determined that the culprit was Jonah.

In chapter 1, verse 8, we read that they found him below deck and woke him up:

> Then they said to him, "Please tell us! For whose cause is this trouble upon us? What is your occupation? And where do you come from? What

is your country? And of what people are you?"

In other words, "Hey, man, what planet are you from? Who in the world are you to cause a storm like this?"

Jonah's answer, however, did nothing to comfort them. He replied, "I am a Hebrew; and I fear the LORD, the God of heaven, who made the sea and the dry land" (verse 9).

They had heard of this God, Yahweh, or Jehovah, and at the mention of His name they "were exceedingly afraid" (verse 10). This was the God who parted seas and drowned great armies. This was the God who made fire fall from the heavens and even raised the dead. Why in the world would their passenger—Jonah—want to run from a God this powerful?

The same question could be asked of us. Why would we run from God? Because sometimes we do, don't we?

Sadly, Jonah had lost his testimony. Verse 10 said that they knew he was running from God. At that point he was a fugitive, not a prophet of the living God. Those sailors must have been thinking, *What's wrong with you? You serve such an awesome God, famous all over the world! Why aren't you following Him and doing what He wants you to do? It's pretty clear that He has a personal interest in you to cause a storm like this!*

Jonah had lost his power, and these pagan seamen were calling him on it. The one person on the whole ship who had the right God wasn't in fellowship with Him and couldn't help them in their great crisis. In His Sermon on the Mount, Jesus said, "If the salt loses its saltiness, how can it be made salty again? It is no longer good for anything, except to be thrown out and trampled underfoot" (Matthew 5:13, NIV).

It reminds me of someone going into a coffee shop and ordering a decaf soy latte. That's just not right. It's as phony as a tofu hamburger. If you're going to order stuff like that, I don't even want to be there. I think people should drink real coffee, with real milk, and eat real hamburgers—not some flat, pale, tasteless imitation of reality.

In the same way, I think the church today has too many decaf disciples. We're losing our power and our authenticity. We are cheap imitations of what we really ought to be in Christ.

Jonah found himself confronted by some angry, terrified sailors who knew he was a prophet on the run and were calling him out on it. Sometimes I think nonbelievers have a better idea of how a believer should behave than a believer has. You will hear people say, "You call yourself a Christian, and yet you act like that?"

Before He went to the cross, Jesus had told people again and again that He would be crucified and then rise again from the dead. Some took that as a warning, and others, like His disciples, took it as a promise.

But here's the strange thing. After it actually happened, His own followers were devastated, disorganized, and disoriented. They lost all hope and scattered. Some of the nonbelievers, however, remembered what Jesus had said before He died. In Matthew 27, some of the Lord's enemies said, "We remember what that deceiver once said while he was still alive: 'After three days I will rise from the dead.' So we request that you seal the tomb until the third day" (verses 63-64, NLT).

The nonbelievers, then, remembered Jesus' promise, but the disciples apparently forgot it.

It reminds me of a true story I read about a tavern that was under construction in a town in Texas. A local church started a campaign—with petitions and prayer meetings—to try and stop the bar from being built. Work, however, progressed on the building. With the grand opening just one week away, the bar was hit by lighting and burned to the ground.

Incensed by this turn of events, the tavern owner sued the church, claiming that they were responsible for the destruction because of their prayers. The church, however, denied any responsibility and any connection between their prayers and the subsequent fire.

When the case went to court, the judge read both the plaintiff's complaint and the defendant's reply. After a few moment's consideration, here is what the judge actually said: "I don't know how I will decide this, but it appears from the paperwork that we have a bar owner who believes in the power of prayer and an entire church congregation that now does not!"

In Jonah's ship, battered by the wind and waves, the pagan sailors were terrified when they learned that the prophet was on the run from the God of Israel. One version says,

> The men were terribly frightened when they heard this. "Oh, why did you do it?" they shouted. "What should we do to you to stop the storm?" For it was getting worse and worse. (Jonah 1:10-11, TLB)

These seamen may not have had a relationship with the God of Israel, but they believed in Him and feared Him.

Sometimes I think this element—the fear of the Lord—is lacking in our churches today. We've become so concerned about relating to our culture and being relevant that we have forgotten to tell people about the awesome, powerful God we serve. In some cases we have traded reverence for relevance.

Church used to be a very staid place where you were expected to dress a certain way, speak in hushed tones in "the sanctuary," and show respect for the Word of God and the worship of God. In many contemporary churches, the pendulum has swung a long way from those days. Our music has changed, styles of worship have changed, and everyone is a lot more casual in their approach to church.

Much of the transformation has been good, but . . . we can also carry it too far. In some churches it's all about having fun, being entertaining, and making everyone feel comfortable and accepted.

Again, that's fine to a degree. But if we lose the sense of a holy, awesome God, and if we water down the clear teaching of the Word of God, we've gone too far.

If a nonbeliever comes into the church I pastor, listens to my sermons, and is never bothered by anything at all, then I may not be doing my job. My task as a pastor is to comfort the afflicted and afflict the comfortable. I want the nonbeliever to say, "Greg, I liked your message to a certain point, but then you said something that really bothered me."

Good! A nonbeliever should be bothered when he realizes that he is lost and that he has offended a holy God. And a believer should be bothered when the Word of God strikes a nerve, and she realizes that her heart or her lifestyle needs a major adjustment. That's what is supposed to happen. As the writer to the Hebrews tells us, "The word of God is alive and powerful. It is sharper than the sharpest two-edged sword, cutting between soul and spirit, between joint and marrow. It exposes our innermost thoughts and desires" (Hebrews 4:12, NLT).

There's nothing casual, comfortable, or laid-back about *that.*

God Uses Imperfect People

Evidently Jonah imagined that he would escape from God and the assignment to preach in Nineveh, one way or another. If the Lord wouldn't let him escape on a ship to Tarshish, Jonah imagined that he would escape through being drowned at sea. When the sailors asked him how to stop the storm, he offered them a quick solution: "Just throw me overboard."

> Then they said to him, "What shall we do to you that the sea may be calm for us?"—for the sea was growing more tempestuous.
>
> And he said to them, "Pick me up and throw me into the sea; then the sea will become calm for you. For I know that this great tempest is because of me." Nevertheless the men rowed hard to return to land, but they could not, for the sea continued to grow more tempestuous against them. (Jonah 1:11-13)

At this point, I don't think Jonah had any inkling about the amazing way that God was prepared to deliver him. In his mind he was probably thinking, "There needs to be a sacrifice here."

This is a picture of what Jesus did for us. For any of us ever to be right with God, there had to be a sacrifice—and Jesus was that final sacrifice, which was acceptable to God. It's no stretch to compare Jesus to Jonah because the Lord used the comparison Himself, as we have already seen.

Eventually the sailors gave up trying to rescue themselves and took advantage of Jonah's final sacrifice. They threw him in—and the storm instantly stopped in its tracks.

> Therefore they cried out to the LORD and said, "We pray, O LORD, please do not let us perish for this man's life, and do not charge us with innocent blood; for You, O LORD, have done as it pleased You." So they picked up Jonah and threw him into the sea, and the sea ceased from its raging. Then the men feared the LORD exceedingly, and offered a sacrifice to the LORD and took vows.
> (Jonah 1:14-16)

Note that they offered a sacrifice to the Lord, the God of Israel, and not to their false gods. It shows that God can still work through flawed people.

Shortly after my wife Cathe became a Christian at age fifteen, she stopped going to church, went back to her old ways, walked away from the Lord, and began smoking pot with her friends. In fact, she had gotten to the point where she was actually mocking Christians.

One day she was in Laguna Beach with one of her non-Christian friends. As they were talking, Cathe saw someone walk by carrying a Bible, and it reminded her of her life as a Christian.

"I used to be a Christian," she told her friend. "I used to walk with the Lord." And then she began describing to her friend how wonderful it was, how the peace of God had filled her heart, and how she had experienced so much joy. She described how she would go to church with other believers and worship the Lord with them.

As her friend listened, she suddenly turned to Cathe and said, "I want that. I want what you used to have. How can I have a relationship with God?" So right there in Laguna Beach, Cathe led her nonbelieving friend to the Lord, and in the process she recommitted her own life to the Lord.

In the same way, even though Jonah was running from God, as a result of his flawed but still effective testimony, the sailors on that ship believed in and feared the God of Israel. God worked through Jonah, even though he was running from God's will. It's great news to know that God can use imperfect, often-failing people.

The Great Fish

No one really knows what Jonah was thinking as he slid

beneath the stormy waters of the sea. Whatever his thoughts might have been, they probably didn't include the fact that God had a custom-designed watercraft moving in his direction to rescue him:

> Now the LORD had prepared a great fish to swallow Jonah. And Jonah was in the belly of the fish three days and three nights. (Jonah 1:17)

Here the word *prepared* means "ordained" or "called."

Was this a great fish or a whale? The Bible really doesn't specify. Some have speculated that it was a sperm whale. Some years ago, researchers found a beached fifty-foot sperm whale with a forty-foot-long giant squid in its stomach. The squid weighed over 440 pounds and was completely intact. If a whale like that could ingest a gigantic squid, then it would be able to handle a small Hebrew prophet just fine! Jonah would have been nothing more than an appetizer.

When Jesus mentioned the "great fish" in Matthew 12, the word for *fish* could be translated "sea monster." It may have been a fish, and it may have been a whale. Frankly, it doesn't matter whether there are no fish in existence today large enough to hold a man for three days. We only need to know there was one.

Jonah was inside the digestive tract of the great fish for

three days and three nights before he finally prayed. That gives you just a little idea of how stubborn he was. There he was, in utter darkness with the stench of fish and digestive fluids, fish slapping him in the face, and seaweed wrapped all around him. Yet he held out for three days before turning to the Lord.

Nevertheless, stubborn as he may have been, Jonah was a child of God, and eventually he broke down and cried out to the Lord.

Sometimes people will make a profession of faith and then seemingly fall away. We ask ourselves, "Did this person lose his salvation?"

My question, in turn, would be, "Was he ever really saved to begin with?"

If someone commits her life to Christ—and then walks away and never comes back, I would suggest to you that she never was a Christian at all. If, on the other hand, someone commits her life to the Lord, walks away, and then comes back to Christ, I would suggest to you that she simply was a prodigal.

The true test is where a person ends up.

A true believer always will come home to the Lord, eventually. A person who is not a true believer won't. In 1 John 2:19 we read, "They went out from us, but they did not really belong to us. For if they had belonged to us, they would have remained with us; but their going showed that none of them belonged to us" (NIV).

My own mother spent most of her life running from God. She was raised in the church as a believer but ran from the Lord as a young woman. Many years later, shortly before she died, God got her attention, and she recommitted her life to Christ. She was a prodigal who came home.

Prayer in a Strange Place

One immediate lesson for us in Jonah's prayer from the fish's belly is that we can call out to God wherever we are. We can pray in any position, any time, and at any place. We can pray privately, publicly, verbally, or silently. We can be kneeling, standing, sitting, lying down, or even driving (but let's keep our eyes open).

When you think about it, bowing our heads and closing our eyes in prayer is a funny custom. Have you ever been with a group of people who were praying, and as the prayer goes on for a while, you open your eyes and look around? Then you notice someone else with their eyes open, and you feel a little bit guilty, almost like you were caught cheating. The truth is, God doesn't care much how you pray, as long as you do.

When Cathe and I pray before a meal, we will tell our granddaughters, "Close your eyes, fold your hands, and let's pray." One day I looked up from our prayer to see my granddaughter Stella with her eyes closed, stuffing a French fry into her mouth. I have to admit that I laughed out loud.

Again, if Jonah prayed in a fish's stomach, you and I can pray anywhere. Daniel prayed in a lion's den. David prayed in a field. Nehemiah prayed as he stood before the king of Persia. Peter prayed both on top of and *under* the water. The main thing is to just pray. In Ephesians 6:18, the apostle Paul says, "Pray in the Spirit on all occasions with all kinds of prayers and requests" (NIV).

Jonah's Prayer

The Bible is such a remarkable book. In Jonah 2:1-9, we have the actual words of a prayer by a man in a fish's stomach. Here's what Jonah said:

> I cried out to the LORD in my great trouble,
> and he answered me.
> I called to you from the land of the dead,
> and LORD, you heard me!
> You threw me into the ocean depths,
> and I sank down to the heart of the sea.
> The mighty waters engulfed me;
> I was buried beneath your wild and stormy waves.

Then I said, "O LORD, you have driven me from
your presence.
Yet I will look once more toward your holy
Temple."

I sank beneath the waves,
and the waters closed over me.
Seaweed wrapped itself around my head.
I sank down to the very roots of the mountains.
I was imprisoned in the earth,
whose gates lock shut forever.
But you, O LORD my God,
snatched me from the jaws of death!
As my life was slipping away,
I remembered the LORD.
And my earnest prayer went out to you
in your holy Temple.
Those who worship false gods
turn their backs on all God's mercies.
But I will offer sacrifices to you with songs of praise,
and I will fulfill all my vows.
For my salvation comes from the LORD alone. (NLT)

This is an amazing prayer. What makes it even more remarkable is that the prophet quotes eight times from the book of Psalms, which must have been one of his favorite books. That's why it's so wonderful to memorize Scripture; you never know when you will find yourself in a tight spot and need the comfort and instruction of God's Word.

When I pray, I like to quote the Scriptures. It's not to remind God of what He has said, but it's to remind *me* of what He has said. For instance, if I'm praying for wisdom, I might say, "Lord, You have told me in the book of James that if anyone lacks wisdom, let him ask of God who will give generously and not hold back. Lord, I need that wisdom. Would You provide it for me right now?" (see James 1:5).

If I am praying for someone who needs healing, I might say, "Lord, You promised in Your Word that if there are any sick among us, we are to call for the elders of the church who will pray for this person and anoint him with oil—and the effectual, fervent prayer of a righteous man will avail much" (see James 5:14-16).

So I will cite a promise of God from His Word, stand on that promise, and then pray.

That is what Jonah was doing. He was quoting the Scriptures, even as he began to lose hope. In chapter 2, verse 7, he said, "When I had lost all hope, I turned my thoughts once more to the LORD. And my earnest prayer went to you in your holy Temple" (TLB).

Notice that Jonah didn't really ask to be delivered. He simply started giving praise to God. In verse 9 he said, "I will offer sacrifices to you with songs of praise."

Maybe you are in a situation right now where you would say, "I find it very difficult to give thanks."

Really? Think of Jonah. He was inside a fish's stomach with a bunch of stinking, dead fish and wrapped up with seaweed. Yet He praised the Lord and gave thanks to Him. The Bible doesn't say, "Give thanks to the Lord when you feel good." It says, "Give thanks to the LORD, for *He is* good!" (1 Chronicles 16:34). Give thanks to God because—no matter what our circumstances—He is in control.

Jonah's Second Chance

What happened after Jonah prayed? His situation dramatically changed:

> So the LORD spoke to the fish, and it vomited Jonah onto dry land.
>
> Now the word of the LORD came to Jonah the second time, saying, "Arise, go to Nineveh, that great city, and preach to it the message that I tell you." (Jonah 2:10–3:2)

Jonah had probably wondered whether God ever would use him again. In fact, the Lord certainly was under no obligation to do so. But all of these things transpired in Jonah's life because the Lord loved him.

The Bible is filled with stories of people to whom God

gave second chances. Do you need a second chance? God gave a second chance to Adam and Eve. They had been strictly warned not to eat of that forbidden fruit in the Garden of Eden. But they did it, and with that disobedience, sin entered the world. God could have thrown up His hands and said, "That's it! I'm done. I'm starting over again." Instead, God called out to them, "Where are you?" In essence God was saying, "I know what you have done, but I love you. Where are you? Why are you hiding?"

God gave a second chance to David in the worst season of his life, after he had committed adultery and murder. He was confronted by the prophet Nathan and repented of his sins. Afterward, God gave him productive years as king over Israel. In his latter years, David made plans and gathered the materials for a great temple to the Lord in Jerusalem.

Samson was given a second chance, too. With his long, flowing locks of hair, he was known for his supernatural strength and his ability to vanquish his enemies. But Samson was a he-man with a she weakness. One thing led to another, and he ended up having his hair shaved off and his eyes gouged out by his enemies. It certainly looked like it was curtains for Israel's mighty hero. But one of the great verses in the Bible says, "However, the hair of his head began to grow again after it had been shaven" (Judges 16:22). (By the way, that's the life verse of every bald man.) Samson's hair did grow again, and he was given another chance to avenge himself on his enemies.

Simon Peter failed miserably, denying the Lord when, in His humanity, He needed him the most. Yet when Christ had risen from the dead, an angel at the empty tomb told the women, "But go, tell His disciples—*and Peter*—that He is going before you into Galilee; there you will see Him" (Mark 16:7).

Have you ever noticed that reference? It wasn't, "Go tell His disciples—and James and John." No, it was "Go tell His disciples—and Peter." Why? Because Peter needed hope, and God gave him a second chance. Then, on the shore of the Sea of Galilee, Jesus personally recommissioned Peter (see John 21).

So it was that Jonah, regurgitated and repentant, got his second chance to do God's will. After being pickled in the gastric juices of that great fish, Jonah probably had all the color washed out of his hair, beard, and skin. Did anyone actually see the massive sea monster cruise into shore and upchuck the prophet? The Bible doesn't say. But Jonah's appearance must have made quite an impression on the population of Nineveh.

I find it interesting that after that entire chain of circumstances, God sent Jonah to Nineveh again. It was Nineveh or bust. God said, in effect, "Jonah, we're going back to where I wanted you to go in the first place. You're not getting out of this."

And this time Jonah didn't hesitate. He set out immediately on the road to Nineveh.

Are you at a place in life where you have strayed from God's path and God's best and need a second chance? What do you need to do? As Paul said (Paul McCartney, that is), you need to "get back, get back. Get back to where you once belonged."

Here is what Jesus told the church of Ephesus in the book of Revelation: "Remember therefore from where you have fallen; repent and do the first works, or else I will come to you quickly and remove your lampstand from its place" (Revelation 2:5).

You could sum it up this way: remember, repent, repeat.

Step one is to remember. Earlier in this chapter I mentioned my wife Cathe, who had gone astray from the Lord as a young teenager. But then as she talked to her friend about her former relationship with God and how good it had been, she repented of her wandering and came back to the Lord with all her heart. She got back to where she needed to be and what she needed to do. It may sound simplistic, but that is exactly what you need to do if you have wandered from God. You need to change your mind, come back to Him, and do those things that He wants you to do.

Step two is to repent. Jonah finally admitted that he had made vows to the Lord: "What I have vowed I will make good" (Jonah 2:9, NIV). He determined to stop wandering, to stop his rebellion, and to return to the Lord in obedience.

Step three is to repeat. In other words, get back into the right pattern of life. Return to daily time in the Word of God. Return to regular fellowship with other believers. Return to time set aside for prayer. Return to the practice of sharing your faith whenever the opportunity presents itself. Make these priorities part of your everyday life.

That pattern of willing obedience will bring perspective and joy.

Life won't always be easy, and it won't always make sense according to our understanding, but this will put us back on the path to perspective . . . and joy.

> How sweet are your words to my taste,
> sweeter than honey to my mouth!
> I gain understanding from your precepts
> therefore I hate every wrong path.
> (Psalm 119:103-104, NIV)

CHAPTER 3
THE MESSAGE WE MUST PROCLAIM

I heard the story of an old codger who liked to spend his days fishing on a lake. One afternoon he was out in his boat near the shore, with his line in the water, when he heard a voice.

The voice said, "Hey, you! Pick me up!"

Startled, the old man looked around but couldn't see anyone. Where had the voice come from?

Again he heard the voice: "Hey, you! Yes, *you*! Pick me up!"

Suddenly his eyes rested on a frog sitting on a lily pad.

"Are you talking to me?" the man asked the frog.

"Yes, I am," the frog answered. "Pick me up and kiss me, and I will become the most beautiful woman you have ever seen."

The man reached down, gently picked up the frog, and slipped it into the pocket of his fishing vest.

"Hey!" the frog protested. "Didn't you hear what I said? If you kiss me, I'll become the most beautiful woman you have ever seen. You'll be the envy of all of your friends!"

The old man shrugged, leaving the frog where it was. "At my age," he said, "I would rather have a talking frog."

Talk about missing the point.

And as I stated earlier, I believe that many have missed the point in the book of Jonah. People through the years have fixated so much on Jonah's being swallowed by a fish—and living to tell the story—that they have missed the real message and heartbeat of the book.

The real story of Jonah is about God and second chances. Nineveh, a city renowned for its wickedness, was given a second chance. And Jonah, a man known for his disobedience and rebellion, also was given a second chance.

The result was perhaps the greatest recorded revival in human history.

The ultimate story of Jonah, of course, is that of a great God who showed great love. But as a corollary to that, this little book shows how one man, or one woman, can make a difference. Because Jonah (eventually) did what God called him to do, an entire city—and effectively an entire nation—was changed for the better.

God's Commission (Reprise)

In Jonah, chapter 3, verses 1 through 3, we encounter God's second commission to Jonah and the prophet's prompt response:

> Now the word of the LORD came to Jonah the second time, saying, "Arise, go to Nineveh, that great city, and preach to it the message that I tell you." So Jonah arose and went to Nineveh, according to the word of the LORD.

Let's identify some things we need to know from the story of Jonah.

To reach our culture, we must preach the gospel.

God didn't tell Jonah to go to Nineveh and be a good example or a silent witness. He didn't move into an apartment in Assyria's capital city, telling himself that he would reach the people by just living a godly life and being kind to others. No, God specifically told him to "preach to it the message that I tell you."

When we use the word *preach*, it might make you think that you have to yell at people. But that isn't so. In fact, preaching can be *conversational*.

You can preach through an e-mail.

You can preach through a post on your social media page.

You can preach conversationally.

The emphasis isn't on *volume*, it's on content; it's on verbally communicating the great good news of the gospel. We've been called to do that. The problem is that some churches have moved away from evangelistic preaching and biblical teaching.

If you look at the early church in the book of Acts, the church that turned the world upside down (see Acts 17:6), you will notice that one of their secrets was "they devoted themselves to the apostles' teaching" (Acts 2:42, NIV). In other words, they offered theology without apology, and we should do the same.

When Jesus started His ministry, the Bible tells us that He was a preacher of the Word. Matthew 4:17 says, "From that time Jesus began to preach and to say, 'Repent, for the kingdom of heaven is at hand.'" In Matthew 10:7, He said, "As you go, preach, saying, 'The kingdom of heaven is at hand.'"

Why preach?

Because preaching is God's primary way of reaching lost people. As I stated earlier, if I were God, I probably wouldn't do it this way. God, after all, can do anything. He could write the gospel across the Milky Way in some magnificent way that no one in all the earth would miss: *BELIEVE IN ME NOW*. For that matter, God could appear to every individual on the planet and say, "Believe in Jesus Christ, and you will be saved." Or, He could raise up an army of mighty angelic beings to go around the world proclaiming the gospel.

And yet, God chose to reach people through ordinary, flawed people like you and me who faithfully share the gospel through our words.

Trust me when I tell you that the *last* thing I ever wanted to be in life was a preacher. When I was a boy, I used to spend time at Corona del Mar beach in Newport Beach, California. Sometimes a man would show up there dressed head-to-toe in black: black coat, black vest, black pants, black hat . . . and holding a big, black Bible. He would stand out in the blazing sun, the sweat pouring down his face, preaching to whomever walked by, telling us that we needed to believe in Jesus. I remember thinking, *This guy is nuts. I would never want to do what he is doing.*

After I became a Christian, however, I discovered the power of verbally articulating the gospel. It seemed so strange to me because I had never done well in speech classes and dreaded the idea of getting up in front of people and talking. I imagined myself to be a behind-the-scenes kind of person. As time went on, however, I began to discover the power in simply proclaiming the message of Christ.

We are to preach the message He has given.

In Jonah 3:2 the Lord told Jonah, "Go to Nineveh . . . and preach to it *the message that I tell you*" (emphasis added).

From what we see in the text, it seems that Jonah started out for Nineveh before he even knew what that specific message would be. But he knew that when the time came,

God would give him the words that He wanted proclaimed to the Ninevites.

In 1 Corinthians 11:23 the apostle Paul said, "For I pass on to you what I received from the Lord himself" (NLT).

Nothing will go *through* you until it has first happened to you. It is a great thing to go through the Word of God, but it is a greater thing when the Word of God has gone through you. To say it in another way, it is not how you mark your Bible but how your Bible marks you.

Jonah was a changed man. He was a resurrection man who effectively had been brought back to life from the very gates of death. As he got that message out, it resonated with the people.

When it comes to presenting the gospel of Christ, it is not for us to tamper with or edit that life-giving message. We don't have to concern ourselves with skipping over certain things or leaving things out for fear of offending someone. By the same token, we don't need to add to the message because we think the Bible needs more of this or that.

Don't tamper with the message of the Scriptures.

Don't toy with the message of the gospel.

Our job is to simply deliver it.

The fact is, there is raw, explosive power in the essential gospel message. Paul says in Romans 1:16, "For I am not ashamed of the gospel of Christ, for it is the power of

God to salvation for everyone who believes."

The word Paul used there for "power" comes from the Greek word *dunamis*, from which we get our English word *dynamite*. To loosely paraphrase, Paul was affirming there is dynamic, explosive power in the message of the gospel. Our job isn't to make the Bible relevant; it is eternally relevant. It is as relevant and applicable today as it was two thousand years ago.

When I step up to the pulpit as a pastor, I'm not preoccupied with thoughts of, *How can I make this interesting?* or *How can I engage people with the message right now?*

No, my job is to simply present the Word of God as clearly as I know how because it is *already* powerful, *already* relevant, and *already* effective. Again, the book of Hebrews tells us that the Word of God "is full of living power: it is sharper than the sharpest dagger, cutting swift and deep into our innermost thoughts and desires with all their parts, exposing us for what we really are" (Hebrews 4:12, TLB).

I know very well that the message of the Bible will do what God wants it to do. My job is to let the lion out of the cage.

Jonah was one in a line of prophets who spoke for God. In other Old Testament books, we read about Isaiah, Jeremiah, Elijah, Ezekiel, and Daniel. In the book of Acts, we read that in the last days "your sons and daughters shall prophesy" (Acts 2:17). Do we have prophets today like there were in the days of the Old Testament? I don't know that we do. But I do know that God speaks to people through people. A literal definition of prophesying is to speak for another.

Let's think for a moment about that and apply it to our lives.

Jonah was God's prophet to speak to his culture. You are, in a sense, God's prophet, or representative, to speak to our culture. Let's see what we can learn from what Jonah did that will help us in what we do.

Becoming God's Spokesperson

1. God's representative, or prophet, is usually an ordinary person.

Isn't that a relief? Ordinary is what most of us are. God seems to go out of His way to use unremarkable, unlikely candidates to proclaim His message. Why? So that He will receive the glory. God isn't looking for flawless, fearless people. He isn't holding out for perfect candidates.

Think about Elijah. At one moment he was on Mount Carmel, challenging the prophets of Baal and winning a contest of faith as the Lord God answered his prayers with fire falling from Heaven. The next moment we see him running like a scared jackrabbit and hiding in a cave because Jezebel the queen had put out a contract on his life. One day he was fearless, and the next day he was fearful.

And yet God used him in a mighty way. The apostle James tied a ribbon around the story by reminding us that "Elijah was as completely human as we are" (James 5:17, TLB).

Sometimes prophets are least appreciated in their own homes. Jesus said, "A prophet is not without honor except in his own country and in his own house" (Matthew 13:57). When Jesus went to His hometown of Nazareth, the text says that He could do no mighty works there because of the unbelief of the people.

Of course, we know that God can do what He wants where He wants when He wants. Yet we read that He did no miracle in His hometown of Nazareth. Why?

They didn't believe in Him.

Why didn't they believe in Him?

Because they had known Him growing up, before He began His ministry. Their minds refused to see Him as anything more than a local boy who had acquired some fame.

The fact is, the hardest people you will ever try to reach are the people in your own home. The hardest people to touch with the gospel are those who are close to you and have known you for years. That includes your own brothers, sisters, parents—and sometimes your own children. Even the Lord didn't effectively reach His own family until He was crucified and rose from the dead.

Bottom line, a prophet who speaks for God most often

will be an ordinary person who may very well be overlooked or scorned by those who know him or her best.

2. God's representative, or prophet, is speaking for Someone Else.

The words you share are not your own.

When I was growing up, I spent some time as a newspaper boy. Nowadays, it's often adults who deliver the papers, and it's done mostly from their cars. But when I was a little boy, I would do my route on my bike. Thankfully, I had a very cool bike. It was a purple Sting-Ray bicycle, with a banana seat and a little roll bar on the back. The back tire was wide, and the front tire was a bit smaller. You might say that it was a bicycle version of a chopper.

The best feature on my bike was a stick shift. I would cruise around on my purple Schwinn Sting-Ray, with canvas bags hanging from it to hold my newspapers. As time went on, I got pretty good at flinging those papers and putting them right where they needed to go. Some homes were easy, and I could loft the paper and have it land right on the front porch. Other homes were more challenging because of trees or a hedge. I had to learn how to toss the paper over obstacles—even with a sideways flip.

But that's what I did every day. I was a delivery boy. My job wasn't to make the news or write the news or edit the news; my job was to *deliver* the news.

That is what we are. We're delivery boys or delivery girls. We've been given the job of delivering the message that God has given to us. It is *His* message. If the message is rejected, we don't take it personally. By the same token, if our message is accepted, we don't take that personally, either.

Sometimes when I speak for the Lord and stand on the Word of God, I am opposed, criticized, or even insulted. Sometimes people will tell lies about me and put out false information about me. I accept that. I already know that is the way it will be, so I'm not shocked when it happens. I choose to speak for the Lord and for His Word, even though Jesus told me that a certain amount of persecution would follow that commitment. But I don't take the criticism personally. I realize that it is a response to the power of the message. And if people respond to the message and give their lives to Christ, I don't take that personally, either.

In other words, I don't take the blame, and I don't take the credit.

Years ago I had the privilege of joining Billy Graham at a crusade he was doing in Portland, Oregon. It was an amazing crusade with an almost revival-like atmosphere in that very liberal city.

I remember one night in particular when God seemed to really bless Billy's message, with many people coming to Christ.

We left the stadium together in a car, with Billy's longtime friend T. W. Wilson driving, while I rode shotgun. Billy and his son Franklin were in the backseat.

As we were pulling out of the parking lot, I leaned over the backseat and said, "That was a great message tonight, Billy."

Billy looked at me with those steel-blue eyes and said, "It's just the gospel."

I turned around, feeling a little awkward. I was just trying to be friendly. I remember thinking to myself, *That didn't go very well. I will say something else*. Turning back around again, I said, "Billy, I love the point when you said that Christ will resensitize your conscience. That was a great point."

Again Billy looked at me and said, "Well, He can!"

I didn't turn around again on the ride back to the hotel. What I learned that night was that you couldn't pin a compliment on Billy Graham. It was like water off a duck's back, and he really didn't want to hear it. His attitude was, "I just did my job. I'm a delivery boy, and I gave the message. Now the results are in the hands of God."

As God's spokespeople, we don't take the credit, and we don't take the blame. We just deliver the goods. And that brings me to a third point.

3. God's representative, or prophet, recognizes that the results are up to the Lord, not up to us.

When our team does a Harvest crusade in a given city, we do everything we can to achieve outstanding results. We put every effort into what we do, with great attention to detail. Most importantly, we put a lot of effort into prayer. We organize people to pray—especially for those who come to the event and don't yet know the Lord.

When the time comes for me to step into the pulpit, I don't feel pressure to gain impressive "results." I will do the best I know how, leaning on the Lord, but I know that it is His job to save people—not mine. I just have to deliver the message. Sometimes the response will be large, like it was with Peter on the day of Pentecost when three thousand people believed. Then again, sometimes the response will be relatively small, as it was for Paul when he preached to all the intellectuals on Mars Hill and only a handful believed.

The simple fact is, God doesn't require success. He requires faithfulness.

Ultimately, what we want to hear the Lord say to us is, "Well done, good and faithful servant." Our job is to simply deliver the message with which we have been entrusted and leave the results in the hands of God.

The Message

Another thing I will add about Jonah is that once he chose to obey the Lord, he got right after it and didn't procrastinate. Once he understood that God was giving him a second chance to do His will, he immediately set out to do it.

Here's what we read in Jonah 3:1-4:

> Now the word of the LORD came to Jonah the second time, saying, "Arise, go to Nineveh, that great city, and preach to it the message that I tell you." So Jonah arose and went to Nineveh, according to the word of the LORD. Now Nineveh was an exceedingly great city, a three-day journey in extent. And Jonah began to enter the city on the first day's walk. Then he cried out and said, "Yet forty days, and Nineveh shall be overthrown!"

Jonah had a very specific message entrusted to Him from God. He didn't have to wonder or agonize about what he would preach in that vast cosmopolitan city; God had told him exactly what to say.

Having looked at the role of the messenger earlier in the passage, let's take a moment now to consider the message we must deliver. Here are the marks of an authentic and accurate message.

The message must be delivered with urgency.

Verse 4 tells us that Jonah "cried out."

It wasn't the first time he'd done so. He also cried out from the stomach of the fish. Back in Jonah 2:1-2 we read, "I cried out to the LORD because of my affliction, and He answered me. Out of the belly of Sheol I cried, and You heard my voice."

Jonah took the desperation he had felt in the stomach of the fish and applied it to the message he gave to the Ninevites. Effectively he was saying, "God gave me a second chance, and God wants to give you a second chance, too!" I believe there was passion in his delivery. He cared, and he cried his message aloud.

Do you care? Does it matter to you what happens to people here on earth and after they enter eternity? The great British preacher C. H. Spurgeon once said, "Winners of souls must first be weepers of souls."[1]

Don't ever kid yourself on this score. *People can tell if you care*. If you are robotic in the way that you share the gospel, you probably won't move many people. You need to put a little heart into it, a little compassion. That will speak volumes to the individual you're sharing with.

Jonah cried out. When he delivered that message, it was with passion. He certainly hadn't cared about the Ninevites before, and as we will see, it was obvious that he didn't care much for them later, when he was wishing judgment upon them. But in that moment, perhaps remembering his own deliverance from death, I believe that he cried out with all his might.

We need to pray that God would give us a deep concern for men and women outside of Christ. You could study apologetics and evangelism techniques for years, but none of that would really matter if you didn't care about lost people.

I can well imagine there was great authenticity in Jonah's voice after all he'd been through. As I mentioned earlier, he was probably washed an unnatural, ghostly white from the gastric juices of the great fish. On top of that, he must have *reeked* like a great fish. He was like a walking fish market, and you could probably pick up the scent when he was blocks away. People probably smelled him before they saw him and asked each other, "What is that odor? And who is that strange-looking white dude coming our way?"

Whatever he may have looked like or smelled like, his message had a ring of authenticity about it. The Ninevites knew he was for real. They could sense it.

A. W. Tozer said, "The world is waiting to hear an authentic voice, a voice from God—not an echo of what others are doing and saying, but an authentic voice."[2]

Authenticity speaks to people. It always has, and it always will.

The message must be clear and definite.

Any child could understand the message that Jonah was delivering: "Forty days, and Nineveh shall be overthrown!"

No one needed a college education to get the point of that message.

Our Lord told us that we must become as little children to enter the kingdom of Heaven (see Matthew 18:3). I love being around kids with their childlike simplicity. It's fun telling stories to my grandkids and seeing the way they engage and listen. When I tell them Bible stories, trying to bring it down to their level, they get it. They understand the stories.

The Bible—and the gospel in particular—is not simplistic, but it is simple. Far too often, I fear, we overcomplicate it, adding things to it that don't really belong or taking things out of it that we think might be offensive to people.

The truth is, we should just proclaim it, in all its simple power. Remember what Paul admitted to the church at Corinth?

> Dear brothers, even when I first came to you I didn't use lofty words and brilliant ideas to tell you God's message. For I decided that I would speak only of Jesus Christ and his death on the cross. I came to you in weakness—timid and trembling. And my preaching was very plain, not with a lot of oratory

> and human wisdom, but the Holy Spirit's power was in my words, proving to those who heard them that the message was from God. I did this because I wanted your faith to stand firmly upon God, not on man's great ideas. (1 Corinthians 2:1-5, TLB)

How well did that simple, passionate preaching work out for Jonah? In Jonah 3:5 we read, "So the people of Nineveh believed God." Notice that it doesn't say they believed Jonah. No, they believed God. The greatest revival in the history of the world came to Nineveh because Jonah delivered God's message and not what people wanted to hear.

This might surprise you a little, but there was an element of hope in this message. Someone may say, "Really? Forty days until destruction? How was that hopeful?"

But it could have been forty hours or even forty minutes. For that matter, God could have leveled the city without any warning at all. Yet in His love and His mercy, God gave them warning, giving them time to repent and a final opportunity to change their hearts and their ways. He gave them forty days of mercy . . . forty days to pray and to cry out to God.

We are effectively doing the same thing when we proclaim the gospel. John 3:16 sums it up: "For God so loved the world that He gave His only begotten Son, that whoever believes in Him should not perish but have everlasting life."

That's really the gospel in a nutshell. If I had to pick one verse in the Bible that summed up the whole gospel, I would pick that one. You have the message of love there: "For God so loved the world that He gave." You also have a warning of judgment: "Whosoever believes in Him should not perish." In other words, if you don't believe this message, you will perish, but if you do, then you won't perish.

Romans 6:23 accomplishes the same thing. It begins with a warning: "For the wages of sin is death." But it follows with a message of hope and forgiveness: "But the gift of God is eternal life in Christ Jesus our Lord."

Frankly, whenever God gives a warning, that is a *good* sign. Sodom and Gomorrah really had no warning. Angels had to drag Lot and his family out of the city just minutes before fire fell from Heaven.

I believe the Lord has been graciously, patiently warning the United States of America to turn back to Him. I also believe that, as a whole, we haven't been paying attention to His warnings. It makes you wonder what it will take to wake up our nation.

If God could bring a mighty revival in Nineveh with no better representative than Jonah and no more gospel than the shouted warnings he preached in their streets, the Lord could surely do the same for America. And God wants you and me to have a part in that.

Preach the Gospel

It's my opinion that most Americans have never heard an accurate presentation of the gospel of Jesus Christ.

Someone might say, "Greg, I have to disagree with you. There are preachers everywhere—on TV, on the radio, on the Internet."

I would acknowledge there is a lot of "God talk" out there. What I said was that I don't think most Americans have heard an accurate *presentation* of the gospel.

If I only tell people that God loves them, then I have not given them the gospel. If I only tell people that God wants to judge them, then I have not really given them the whole gospel. There are elements that must be in place for the gospel to be the gospel; if those elements are left out, then it is no longer the gospel. It would be like making a chocolate cake without chocolate. Certain ingredients must be there for the chocolate cake to be a chocolate cake. The same is true of the gospel.

What are those elements? First of all we have to recognize what the word *gospel* means. A literal definition of the term means "good news." Before we can fully appreciate the good news, however, we have to first understand the bad news. If I don't tell people the bad news as well as the good news, then I could be guilty of offering to them a "different gospel" or a "counterfeit gospel."

In Galatians 1:6-7 Paul wrote, “I am astonished that you are so quickly deserting the one who called you to live in the grace of Christ and are turning to a different gospel—which is really no gospel at all. Evidently some people are throwing you into confusion and are trying to pervert the gospel of Christ” (NIV).

What does that mean? They were adding things to the gospel that do not belong.

What Is the Gospel?

Let’s break it down. Let’s start with the bad news, before we give the good news. And here it is: We are all sinners. Every one of us has sinned—sometimes in ignorance but usually on purpose. Romans 3:23 says, “All have sinned and fall short of the glory of God.” First John 1:8 tells us that “if we say we have no sin, we deceive ourselves, and the truth is not in us.”

God has given us the Ten Commandments. Why? So that if we live by these rules, we will become holy people? No. In fact, it’s the very opposite. The Ten Commandments are like a moral mirror; I look at them and realize I fall short. The Ten Commandments both open my eyes and shut my mouth.

Sometimes people will say, “Don’t call me a sinner. I am not a sinner.”

In response I will ask, "Have you ever lied? Have you ever stolen anything? Have you ever taken the Lord's name in vain? Have you ever committed adultery?"

They usually will admit to one or two of those things. Then I will remind them that if they have committed any of these sins, even one of them, they are sinners before God. In James 2:10 we read that "whoever keeps the whole law and yet stumbles at just one point is guilty of breaking all of it" (NIV).

Someone might say, "I'm a good person. I live a good life. I believe that one day I will stand before God, and He will let me into Heaven."

Honestly, there are some good people out there doing some good things. I've met nonbelievers who live better lives than some Christians I know. I've met nonbelievers who are kind and trustworthy. They're stand-up people, the kind of people you would like to spend time with.

Some nonbelievers have been great humanitarians, doing wonderful work for the poor and disadvantaged of the world. Others have been courageous heroes—soldiers and firefighters and police officers—who literally lay down their lives to protect others. There's no denying these things.

Our definition of good, however—the way we see people and value their positive, even noble, traits—has very little to do with a holy God's eternal standards. The Bible says, "There is no one righteous, not even one; there is no one who understands; there is no one who seeks God. All have turned away, they have together become worthless; there is no one who does good, not even one" (Romans 3:10-12, NIV).

In general there is no good in man that can satisfy a holy and righteous God.

People outside of Christ may say good and worthy words and perform good and worthy actions, but human goodness never will be enough to open the doors to Heaven and give us a relationship with God.

God has set the bar very high. He says, "Be holy, for I am holy" (1 Peter 1:16).

But we're not. You are not holy. Nor am I. In myself, I fall short of that mark. *Way* short. The distance between God and Greg Laurie is so vast, I never could reach (not in a million years) to His level.

That is the bad news—that I am a sinner, separated from God.

But here is the great *good* news. In fact, it's the best news that ever was:

> When we were utterly helpless, Christ came at just the right time and died for us sinners. Now, most people would not be willing to die for an upright person, though someone might perhaps be willing to die for a person who is especially good. But

> God showed his great love for us by sending Christ to die for us while we were still sinners. And since we have been made right in God's sight by the blood of Christ, he will certainly save us from God's condemnation. (Romans 5:6-9, NLT)

Maybe someone reading these pages is saying, "But Greg, this is so basic! Why are you including this?" It's because I have seen so many gospel presentations that leave out this progression from bad news to good news. They don't tell a person that he or she is a sinner for fear of offense. But if we don't tell the truth, we will offend God! This is the gospel. We have to tell people the whole truth. A man or woman outside of Christ is a sinner, hopelessly separated from God. But Jesus Christ died on a cross to pay the penalty for our sins and to open up the way to Heaven and eternal life.

In every gospel presentation we need to make a beeline to the cross.

As Paul told the Corinthians, "I resolved to know nothing while I was with you except Jesus Christ and him crucified" (1 Corinthians 2:2, NIV).

The Good News is embodied in Jesus Christ. Jesus Himself said, "I am the way, the truth, and the life. No one comes to the Father except through Me" (John 14:6).

The apostle Peter echoed the same thought in Acts 4:12 when he said, "Nor is there salvation in any other, for there is no other name under heaven given among men by which we must be saved."

The apostle Paul highlights that truth again, in 1 Timothy 2:5-6: "For there is one God and one Mediator between God and men, the Man Christ Jesus, who gave Himself a ransom for all."

The gospel, in a nutshell, is that Christ died for your sins, He was buried, and He was raised again on the third day.

Someone once asked the great British preacher Charles Spurgeon if he could put his Christian faith in a few words. "It is all in four words," he said. "Jesus died for me!"[3]

There is power in the message of the cross, which is the heart of the gospel. That is why Paul said in 1 Corinthians 1:17, "Christ did not send me to baptize, but to preach the gospel, not with wisdom of words, lest the cross of Christ should be made of no effect."

Here is my concern. Sometimes in our attempts to cross over, we don't bring the cross over. Yes, we want to be relevant, and we want to connect with people in our world. But what they need is what every person on earth needs: the authentic gospel of Jesus Christ.

I have one more Billy Graham story. Over lunch one day I asked him this question: "If an older Billy—after all your years of preaching—could speak to a younger Billy, what would you say?"

Here was Billy's answer: "I would preach more on the cross of Christ and the blood because that is where the power is."

What Billy Graham said that day is as true in one-on-one evangelism as it is in preaching. If you bring into your witnessing the bad news of man's lost condition, followed by the good news of Christ's death on the cross for our sins, then you will be armed and dangerous! You will be tapping into the supernatural power of the gospel message.

Sometimes people will say, "But Greg, what if they ask me a question, and I don't know the answer?"

Don't let it throw you! Do your best to answer the question, and if you don't have the answer, say so. Just make sure that you present the gospel, telling that person what Jesus did for him or her. Tell of the death of Christ, the resurrection of Christ, and how much He loves that person.

Again, we don't have to write or edit the news; we're the delivery boys and girls. It's our job to deliver the Good News.

CHAPTER 4
REVIVAL IN OUR TIME

In its day, Nineveh was a megacity with somewhere around a million people—roughly the same as present-day San Francisco.

Nineveh was the capital of the Assyrian Empire, a world superpower at that time. The city itself was so expansive that it took about three days to walk around its perimeter.

Not only was Nineveh a large city, but the Ninevites lived large. They enjoyed the best chariots, the finest foods, and the most exotic entertainment. Nineveh had an extensive business and commercial system like no other in the world. The Assyrian Empire had effectively ruled the world for two hundred years at this point with (what had been) the most powerful army on the planet.

But unbeknownst to them, things were about to change. Babylon was beginning to flex its own military muscle and was on the cusp of overtaking Assyria. Because of this, Nineveh's days were numbered.

But that is true of every nation. Every nation's days are numbered. Every nation has a moment when it is born and a moment when it either dies or is dramatically diminished—and that includes our nation.

God's judgment ultimately will come to America. It's only a matter of time.

Our prayer should be that the Lord would send at least one more great spiritual awakening in our land before that judgment comes.

Do you doubt that this could happen? You shouldn't. If God could bring a mighty revival in a hardened, hostile megacity like Nineveh, then certainly the Lord could do the same for the United States.

Nineveh Responds

On the day Jonah entered the city, he shouted to the crowds: "Forty days from now Nineveh will be destroyed!" The people of Nineveh believed God's message, and from the greatest to the least, they declared a fast and put on burlap to show their sorrow.

When the king of Nineveh heard what Jonah was saying, he stepped down from his throne and took off his royal robes. He dressed himself in burlap and sat on a heap of ashes. Then the king and his nobles sent this decree throughout the city:

> "No one, not even the animals from your herds and flocks, may eat or drink anything at all. People and

> animals alike must wear garments of mourning, and everyone must pray earnestly to God. They must turn from their evil ways and stop all their violence. Who can tell? Perhaps even yet God will change his mind and hold back his fierce anger from destroying us."
>
> When God saw what they had done and how they had put a stop to their evil ways, he changed his mind and did not carry out the destruction he had threatened. (Jonah 3:4-10, NLT)

This is a stunning spiritual awakening, an entire great city turning to God! The Ninevites even turned from those particular sins of cruelty and violence they had been known for all over the world. As a result, God spared them and sent a nationwide spiritual awakening.

Really? To Nineveh? To the cruel Assyrians? This reminds us that no one is beyond the reach of God. The capital city of the Assyrian Empire had been a vile, violent place, and yet God saved them, pulling them back from the very edge of destruction.

Is there someone in your life whom you couldn't, in your wildest dreams, imagine becoming a Christian? When you picture that person carrying around a Bible or saying, "Praise the Lord," it makes you want to laugh out loud because it seems so utterly, ridiculously, impossible to you.

But it isn't ridiculous or impossible at all. God can save that man. God can bring that woman to faith.

You say, "Really, Greg, you have no idea. This person is too hardened (or too addicted . . . or too intellectual . . . or too cynical . . . or too political . . . or too *whatever*)."

But wait a second. The Bible gives us the story of how Saul of Tarsus gave his life to Jesus Christ. This brilliant scholar was a man who hunted down, tortured, and killed Christians for a living. He wasn't just ambivalent or cynical about Christianity; he hated it and had dedicated his life to stamping it out. Yet God got hold of Saul, just as He got hold of Nineveh.

Here is what I would challenge you to do regarding that "impossible-to-reach" individual in your life. Start praying for that person by name, every day, and ask the Lord to save him or her. And pray also that the Lord would give you an open door to simply tell that person what knowing the Lord has meant to your life.

A young pastor once came to see Charles Spurgeon. Spurgeon pastored what we today would call a megachurch, with thousands of people from all over London coming to hear him preach.

"I am a minister of Christ, and I have been preaching for several years, but I have not had much fruits of my preaching," the young pastor complained to Spurgeon. "Yet I believe I preach the truth in a right spirit, but the Lord does not give me souls."

Spurgeon asked him, "You do not expect that every time you preach the gospel the Holy Ghost is coming down upon the people to turn some soul to Jesus Christ, do you?"

"Why, of course not," the young man replied.

"Well, that is just what I thought," Spurgeon told him. "According to your faith be it unto you."[1]

The young pastor had been planning for failure by thinking that no one would respond to the message. Spurgeon was telling him that he needed to attempt great things for God and to expect great things *from* God.

Could God send another spiritual awakening to America? I believe that He could, and I pray that He will.

America's Awakenings

We have had four great spiritual awakenings in our nation's history. The first came in the 1700s, when our country was still in formation, and it was led by men such as Jonathan Edwards and George Whitfield. During just two years of this revival, from 1740 to 1742, between twenty-five thousand and fifty thousand people were added to New England churches. That may not sound like a high number, but consider the fact that the population of the whole nation was only around three hundred thousand at that point.

The Second Great Awakening was from approximately 1790 to 1840 and included preachers like Charles Finney. These were the days of the Wild West when laws were disregarded in various parts of the nation and sexual sin was rampant. At camp meetings around the country, crowds numbering as high as fifteen thousand would gather for several days, and thousands would come to faith. Between 1800 and 1803, more than ten thousand people came to Christ in Kentucky alone.

Sometimes organizers would set up big tents out in a pasture or in the middle of a forest, and thousands of frontier people would come to hear the gospel preached and turn their lives over to the Lord. A lanky young lawyer was known to have attended some of those meetings and had his life impacted by them. We know him as Abraham Lincoln. Lincoln went on to become arguably the most beloved president in American history, second only perhaps to George Washington. President Lincoln's drive to end the scourge of slavery was driven by his Christian views, which became stronger toward the end of his life.

The Third Great Awakening in American history—and one with very unique beginnings—took place from 1857 to 1859. It all began with a forty-eight-year-old businessman named Jeremiah Lamphier, who started a weekly lunch-hour prayer meeting on Fulton Street in New York City in September, 1857. It began slowly but soon exploded. (One of the things that caused it to explode was the crash of the stock market in October.) Before long, prayer meetings were happening everywhere in New York, even filling the theaters on Broadway. Within six months, ten thousand people gathered daily for prayer throughout the city. It is reported that fifty-thousand New Yorkers were converted from March to May, with ten thousand additions to church membership rolls every week during this revival.

As the awakening spread across the country, reported conversions reached an average of fifty thousand a week for a couple of years. All in all, over a million people in America came to Christ during this brief period. One of the men who came out of this amazing national revival was the great evangelist D. L. Moody.

It all started with a modest, lunch-hour prayer meeting for business people and turned into a spiritual tsunami that rolled across the nation.

The Fourth Great Awakening, in my opinion, was the Jesus Movement, which began in the 1960s and continued into the 1970s. These were tumultuous years in our country. In the 1950s and '60s, bomb drills in school classrooms were mandatory. The Cuban Missile Crisis brought us to the brink of a nuclear confrontation with Russia. Not long after that, our nation's young president, John F. Kennedy, was assassinated in Dallas—followed by the assassination of Martin Luther King, Jr. President Kennedy's brother Robert also was assassinated, while he was running for the presidency. This was traumatizing for a nation. The Vietnam War was raging with no end in sight, and the Watergate scandal was about to erupt, which would further erode America's trust in once-revered institutions. American young people were rebelling against society with an intensity that hadn't been seen before. Their mantra was "sex, drugs, and rock and roll." One of the slogans of the time was, "Turn on, tune in, drop out."

Only months after President Kennedy was shot, the Beatles made their appearance on *The Ed Sullivan Show*, watched nationally by an estimated audience of 73 million people. The new youth culture effectively was born in those days.

By and large, the church was ineffective in reaching these kids. John Lennon made his controversial statement around this time that the Beatles were more popular than Jesus. In some ways he was right; for many young people, the Beatles were more popular than Jesus.

And then, inexplicably . . . supernaturally . . . God began to work. Young kids, particularly on the West Coast at first, were coming to Christ by the hundreds—and soon by the thousands. Many of these young people were showing up in some very conservative churches. There was no contemporary Christian music back then, and many churches were straight-laced and didn't approve of long hair, facial hair, bare feet, or casual clothing at church. When all of these "hippie kids" started showing up, some churches welcomed them and experienced revival. Other churches did not welcome them and did not experience revival.

One church that opened its doors to the hippies was Calvary Chapel in Costa Mesa, California. At first Pastor Chuck Smith didn't like the hippies. He thought they all needed to get a haircut and go to work. His wife, Kay, however, had a heart for these young people and prayed for them. She had been specifically praying that the Lord would let her and her husband meet a genuine living, breathing hippie.

Kay's prayers were answered when a young man named Lonnie Frisbee showed up at their house one day. Lonnie had come to Christ in San Francisco. Eventually, Chuck let Lonnie start preaching at Calvary Chapel. Before long, the services included Christian bands, and a whole new genre called contemporary Christian music was launched.

I watched all this happen because I came to Christ in 1970. The Jesus Movement didn't start at Calvary Chapel, but it blew through Calvary Chapel, as it did in many other places. A lot of these kids came to Christ, wanted to know how to grow more in the Lord, and then went out and started planting churches of their own. Our own church, Harvest Christian Fellowship, was born during this revival. I look back today and thank God that He allowed me to be around for that.

But that was forty years ago, and it is *history*. It is a glorious history, but it is history nonetheless. We can't live in the past, but we can learn from it. And what we can do now is to pray for another spiritual awakening, for another Jesus Movement, in our beloved America. There isn't much chance that it will look like the last one, but that doesn't matter. The Lord knows how to reach each generation, and we need to ask that He would. In Psalm 85:6 the psalmist wrote, "Will You not revive us again, that Your people may rejoice in You?" In Habakkuk 3:2 the prophet wrote, "I have heard all about you, LORD. I am filled with awe by your amazing works. In this time of our deep need, help us again as you did in years gone by" (NLT).

We have new generations taking their place in the world, generations that need their own revival, their own awakening. We should pray that the Lord would grace us with another.

What Is Revival?

What is revival? That's a word that has been thrown around for years in Christian circles. Sometimes you will see a church with a sign out front that says, "Revival this week only. Starts at 7:00 p.m. Ends at 9:00 p.m."

Those might be some really good meetings, but I don't know if you could classify them as revivals. Revival isn't something that we do for God; it's something that God does for us. You can't create a revival or *organize* a revival, but you can agonize for a revival in prayer. It is a supernatural invasion of God.

One person defined revival as a community saturated with God. Richard Owen Roberts wrote, "Revival is an extraordinary movement of the Holy Spirit producing extraordinary results."[2] A. W. Tozer defined revival as that which changes the moral climate of a community. The fact is, revival is nothing more or less than a new beginning of obedience to God.

Nonbelievers don't need revival; they need salvation. God's people need revival. The church needs revival. You and I need revival. The word implies being restored to one's original condition—getting back to the place where God wants us to be.

Spurgeon defined the phenomenon like this: "To be revived is a blessing which can only be enjoyed by those who have some degree of life. Those who have no spiritual life are not, and cannot be, in the strictest sense of the term, subjects of a revival . . . *A true revival is to be looked for in the church of God.*"[3]

Revival, then, is for believers only. But evangelism is for nonbelievers, and that is why we do evangelistic crusades. As I said earlier, I don't believe that most Americans have heard an authentic, biblical, gospel invitation. Frankly, I believe that our country is filled with a lot of "almost Christians." They know a little bit about Jesus and the gospel, but they don't fully understand it and have never really embraced it.

Almost. We all hear (or use) that term from time to time. When I'm going somewhere with my wife, I will sometimes say to her, "We have to go now. Are you ready?"

And she might reply, "Almost."

But what does that mean? It might mean another fifteen minutes!

Being an "almost Christian" is no more valid than being "almost pregnant." You either are or you aren't.

The apostle Paul presented the gospel to Herod Agrippa, who was moved by Paul's words. At the end of it, Herod said, "You almost persuade me to become a Christian" (Acts 26:28).

In that moment Herod was an "almost Christian," and America, I believe, is filled with almost Christians. They've heard the gospel, or part of the gospel, but have never responded to it. Our job is to go and preach the message that God has given us, just as Jonah (finally) did in Nineveh.

Jonah's Ugly Moment

One of the reasons I believe the Bible is the Word of God is because it always tells the truth—even if that truth isn't flattering to the subjects. The Bible isn't a puff piece, edited to make its heroes look better. It just tells us what really happened.

If the book of Jonah were a movie, chapter 3 would be a good ending. The reluctant, disobedient prophet, disciplined by the Lord through his ordeal with the great fish, became the instrument God used to turn a great city to the Lord. THE END. Roll the credits!

But that isn't where the book really ends.

If I had written the book of Jonah, I might have found an excuse to leave out this final chapter. Yes, it's honest and real, but it certainly doesn't present Jonah in a very good light.

A great spiritual awakening unlike anything the world had ever seen had broken out in the heart of the evil empire of Assyria. A million lives may have been spared, and thousands turned to the God of Israel for mercy. And how did Jonah respond? Did he rejoice? Did he fall on his face before the Lord in gratitude and wonder?

Not so much. Here is how the Scriptures describe the prophet's less-than-glorious reaction:

> This change of plans greatly upset Jonah, and he became very angry. So he complained to the LORD about it: "Didn't I say before I left home that you would do this, LORD? That is why I ran away

> to Tarshish! I knew that you are a merciful and compassionate God, slow to get angry and filled with unfailing love. You are eager to turn back from destroying people. Just kill me now, LORD! I'd rather be dead than alive if what I predicted will not happen."
>
> The LORD replied, "Is it right for you to be angry about this?" (Jonah 4:1-4, NLT)

Jonah was angry because God didn't wipe out the Ninevites, and God answered him with a simple question. Another translation of God's final statement would be: "You are very angry, aren't you? I can see that by looking at you."

From the original language, the word *angry* used here could be translated "to burn." Jonah was fuming. He should have been rejoicing, and instead he was angry to the bone. Why? Probably because he was so preoccupied with himself and his own prejudices. He was telling the Lord, "I'd rather be dead than see *these people* spared."

This is a little surprising to me. You would think that after the traumatic experiences he had just been through—spending three days and three nights in a fish's stomach and almost dying—he would have had a different, more humble attitude. But no, he went right back to the old arguments he had used with the Lord before he fled for Tarshish.

Sometimes people are concerned about new believers who don't change their lifestyles quickly enough. As a pastor, I'm more concerned with old believers who have stopped changing altogether.

Let me explain. You may know some new believers who have made a commitment to Christ, but their habits, language, and behaviors aren't changing as quickly as you would like them to. They still use profanity now and then, lose their temper, or maybe have a difficult time kicking old habits. Our job is to be patient with them, keep praying for them, and encourage them whenever we can.

My greater concern is with the person who has been a believer for years but has stagnated in his or her walk with Christ and is no longer making changes. This is someone who may have traded in the old sins that he or she used to commit—like immorality, drug abuse, or drinking—and has allowed other "more acceptable" sins such as pride, backbiting, gossip, or bitterness to replace them.

Jonah was an older saint—a follower of the living God—who was having a relapse. He was angry with God and bitter toward Him.

That may be true of you, even as you read this chapter. Maybe at some point you feel that God let you down, that He didn't answer your prayers the way you had hoped, or that events in your life didn't turn out well for you. It could be that in your perceptions, He has blessed someone else more than you, and you feel jealous. Sometimes we wonder why a good God would allow bad things to happen to good people. Jonah was wondering why a good God would allow *good* things to happen to bad people.

He would have been happy if God had chosen to wipe Nineveh off the map. Perhaps still hoping that the Lord would even yet change His mind and punish the Ninevites anyway, he pulled up a ringside seat just outside of town to watch the action:

> Then Jonah went out to the east side of the city and made a shelter to sit under as he waited to see what would happen to the city. (Jonah 4:5, NLT)

All Jonah needed was some popcorn and a Coke (or a box of Milk Duds). Watching a million people die under God's hand—in 3-D Technicolor—would have been great entertainment for him.

> And the LORD God arranged for a leafy plant to grow there, and soon it spread its broad leaves over Jonah's head, shading him from the sun. This eased his discomfort, and Jonah was very grateful for the plant.
>
> But God also arranged for a worm! The next morning at dawn the worm ate through the stem of the plant so that it withered away. (verse 6)

The King James Version calls this leafy plant a gourd. It had leaves like a palm tree, offering ample shade. So Jonah had the comfort of his little shelter and a beautiful tree to keep him shaded and feeling easy. The text says that Jonah was "very grateful" or "very happy" (NIV) about this situation.

Obviously he was more concerned about his own comfort than about the souls of others. We might look down on this attitude, but how often have we had the same warped point of view about our world?

Frankly, this can happen in our lives more easily than we might imagine. We gradually drift away from a vital, day-by-day relationship with the Lord and wake up to find ourselves far from the person we used to be—and far from the heart of God.

Have you found that the Bible is no longer alive to you as it once was? Is prayer no longer a regular part of your life? Have you come to a point where you can't even remember the last time you actually engaged someone in a conversation about Christ? Has your church attendance become erratic? Every one of us has the potential of sacrificing our availability to the Lord for our own personal comforts and agendas.

When that happens, we become like the older brother in the story of the prodigal son (see Luke 15:11-32). As you may remember, he became angry when his younger brother returned home after a season of wild and wasteful living. He didn't want his father to forgive his brother, and he especially didn't want him to celebrate the young man's return home. He was angry about his father's grace, just as Jonah was angry about God's mercy.

Bringing that thought home, are we more concerned about our own comfort and convenience than about the transformation of another person? Are we more wrapped up in what pleases us than in what might change the eternal destiny of someone outside of Christ?

I've heard Christians complaining about evangelistic events like our Harvest Crusades, saying, "I really don't want to invite anyone. I don't like big crowds. The traffic is terrible. And it's not really my style of music."

But these are all issues relating to our personal comfort and preferences. Isn't enduring these discomforts worth seeing a person coming to faith in Christ? It is not about you, and it is not about me. It is about the eternal souls of men and women, boys and girls, who will be lost forever unless they find salvation in Jesus Christ.

I don't think you and I really have much of an idea about the impact in Heaven when one person turns to Christ on earth. In Luke 15, the chapter where Jesus tells the story of the prodigal son, Jesus speaks of "joy in heaven" (verse 7) and "joy in the presence of the angels of God over one sinner who repents" (verse 10).

Every time a person believes in Jesus on earth, there is a party in Heaven. Notice it doesn't say there is joy whenever one hundred people or more repent. Rather, it says there is joy when one repents. One sinner is enough to make Heaven break out in applause. When you think about it, that is worth some effort, discomfort, or even pain to reach that goal.

I remember the Harvest Crusade I spoke at only days after our son Christopher went to Heaven on July 24, 2008. Some people wondered if I would even be there, let alone speak.

But what else could I do? I knew that it was the thing I could do and should do. I knew my son was in Heaven, and I wanted others to have the opportunity to join him there. Was it difficult? I can't even tell you how difficult it was. It was one of the hardest times of my life. And yet God came near to me in a wonderful way during that time. As I saw people come to Christ that year, it was almost as though I could audibly hear the applause of heaven.

What would happen to you or me if God were to open up a portal and give us a glimpse of the other side, allowing us to see into Heaven? What would it be like if we could see our loved ones there, happily enjoying the presence of God and all the joys that await us? How would that impact the way we live our lives right now? And what if God opened up a portal or a window to hell, and we could see what was taking place there? How frightening that would be! How terrible it would be to think, *I know people who could end up there if they don't turn to Christ.*

My point is that we need to think beyond our own temporary comfort and beyond our own personal preferences to consider the eternal destinies of our own neighbors, acquaintances, friends, and family.

Jonah Gets Some Perspective

> And as the sun grew hot, God arranged for a scorching east wind to blow on Jonah. The sun beat down on his head until he grew faint and wished to die. "Death is certainly better than living like this!" he exclaimed.
>
> Then God said to Jonah, "Is it right for you to be angry because the plant died?"
>
> "Yes," Jonah retorted, "even angry enough to die!"
>
> Then the LORD said, "You feel sorry about the plant, though you did nothing to put it there. It came quickly and died quickly. But Nineveh has more than 120,000 people living in spiritual darkness, not to mention all the animals. Shouldn't I feel sorry for such a great city?"
>
> (Jonah 4:8-11, NLT)

The Lord sent a worm to eat Jonah's plant, or gourd, and Jonah practically went out of his gourd as a result. The sun beat down on his head, a hot wind whipped dust into his face, and he didn't have so much as a tube of sunscreen.

"I've had it," he basically told God. "Why don't you just let me die?"

The Lord had spared thousands of lives, and Jonah was still wrapped up in concerns over his own comfort. He had lost his bit of shade over his head, and he acted as though it were the end of the world.

Jonah had been delivered from the belly of a great fish, but he still needed delivering from a narrow, self-centered, hateful attitude. Did his heart eventually change so that he was thinking more like the Lord? I'm guessing it did, because I believe that Jonah went on to write the book of Jonah, where God's compassion (and Jonah's stubborn heart) are on full display.

Heaven rejoices when a sinner believes, and so should we.

Statistics tell us that between 80 and 90 percent of the people who hear a personal gospel presentation receive it from someone who has known the Lord for two years or less. New believers seem to understand the need and urgency more clearly than older, more established believers.

My daughter-in-law Brittni went up to Los Angeles's skid row with a group from our church to work with Fred Jordan Missions (which is led by Willie Jordan, my aunt). Throughout the year, this ministry shares the gospel with people and feeds and clothes them as well.

The group from our church was giving out bottles of water and inviting people to a meal where there would be a gospel presentation. As Brittni was talking to people on the bus, most of whom she had never seen before, she started asking each of them how long they had known the Lord. She told me that almost every person on the bus said, "I just came to Christ" or "I came to Christ a month ago" or "I just accepted Christ the other day."

The bus was filled with new converts who wanted to reach out to hurting people with the gospel. I couldn't help wondering, *Where were the older converts? Where were the people who have walked with Christ for years? Why weren't they there?*

Have we become more concerned with our comfort than with the souls of people? If so, we need to ask God to change our hearts.

Jonah had his Nineveh, but in a sense, each of us has a Nineveh of our own—a place where the Lord wants us to go or a task that the Lord wants us to undertake. Your Nineveh doesn't have to be across the world like Jonah's Nineveh. Your Nineveh might be across town or even across the street. It is a place where God has called you to go, a place where popularity doesn't matter, a place where faithfulness to the will of God is all that really counts.

It may also be a place that leads to a blessing beyond your wildest dreams.

When Jonah was an old man, he could look back on being part of the greatest revival in the history of the world. It hadn't been easy, it hadn't been a textbook evangelistic crusade, and through much of it, Jonah's attitude hadn't been very inspirational or exemplary.

But God had chosen to use him anyway, in spite of his shortcomings. And He will use you in the same way as you make yourself available to go where He asks you to go and say what He asks you to say.

So when the Lord calls, don't say, "Here I am . . . send *him*!"

Rather, say, "Here I am, send me!"

Let's attempt great things for God and expect great things from Him.

NOTES

Chapter 1: Here Am I . . . Send Him!

1. "Roy Riegels," *Wikipedia.com*, accessed April 16, 2014, http://en.wikipedia.org/wiki/Roy_Riegels.
2. Charles R. Swindoll, *Charles R. Swindoll: The Inspirational Writings* (New York: BBS Publishing, 1994), 434.

Chapter 2: The Hard-to-Swallow Truth About Disobedience

1. Warren W. Wiersbe, *The Wiersbe Bible Commentary: New Testament* (Colorado Springs: David C. Cook, 2007), 42.

Chapter 3: The Message We Must Proclaim

1. Charles Spurgeon, quoted in Martin H. Manser, ed., *The Westminster Collection of Christian Quotations* (Louisville, KY: Westminster John Knox Press, 2001), 370.
2. A. W. Tozer, *Rut, Rot, or Revival: The Condition of the Church* (Camp Hill, PA: Christian Publications, 1992), 178.
3. Ernest W. Bacon, *Spurgeon: Heir of the Puritans* (Arlington Heights, IL: Christian Liberty Press, 2001), 114.

Chapter 4: Revival in Our Time

1. A. T. Pierson, *The Heart of the Gospel: Sermons on the Life-Changing Power of the Good News* (Grand Rapids, MI: Kregel Publications, 1996), 31.
2. Richard Owen Roberts, *Revival* (Carol Stream, IL: Tyndale House Publishers, 1982), 16.
3. C. H. Spurgeon, "What Is a Revival?" *The Sword and the Trowel* (London, 1866), 529-530.